High Street to Homestead

High Street to Homestead

ANGELA WILLIAMS
with DEBORAH CODDINGTON

RANDOM HOUSE
NEW ZEALAND

RANDOM HOUSE

UK | USA | Canada | Ireland | Australia
India | New Zealand | South Africa | China

Random House is an imprint of the Penguin Random House group of companies, whose addresses can be found at global.penguinrandomhouse.com.

First published by Penguin Random House New Zealand, 2016

10 9 8 7 6 5 4 3 2 1

Text © Angela Williams, 2016

The right of Deborah Coddington to be identified as the author of this Work in terms of section 96 of the Copyright Act 1994 is hereby asserted.

All rights reserved. Without limiting the rights under copyright reserved above, no part of this publication may be reproduced, stored in or introduced into a retrieval system, or transmitted, in any form or by any means (electronic, mechanical, photocopying, recording or otherwise), without the prior written permission of both the copyright owner and the above publisher of this book.

Cover and text design by Sam Bunny © Penguin Random House New Zealand
Front cover photograph by Tessa Chrisp
Back cover photograph by Neil Gussey/Simply You
Internal photographs © Angela Williams, except for pages 2–3, 6–7, 8, 92, 154, 222–223, 246–247 © Chris Coad and page 29 © Alex Hedley
Printed and bound in Australia by Griffin Press,
an Accredited ISO AS/NZS 14001 Environmental Management Systems Printer

A catalogue record for this book is available from the National Library of New Zealand.

ISBN 978-1-77553-853-0
eISBN 978-1-77553-871-4

penguinrandomhouse.co.nz

Contents

CHAPTER ONE
Night sweats..8

CHAPTER TWO
Reel back the years..20

CHAPTER THREE
Nothing new under the Te Parae sun..........................30

CHAPTER FOUR
Thoroughbred stud once more?...................................40

CHAPTER FIVE
Horses, my passion..50

CHAPTER SIX
Let us entertain you...62

CHAPTER SEVEN
Wedding days...74

CHAPTER EIGHT
Selling handbags..80

CHAPTER NINE
Home to stay..92

CHAPTER TEN
My big OE..104

CHAPTER ELEVEN
Scotland..114

CHAPTER TWELVE
Down South..120

CHAPTER THIRTEEN
Mark..126

CHAPTER FOURTEEN
Melbourne..144

CHAPTER FIFTEEN
Where to start?..154

CHAPTER SIXTEEN
Miss New Zealand and Biggles...............................164

CHAPTER SEVENTEEN
Organised chaos...176

CHAPTER EIGHTEEN
My Te Parae...196

CHAPTER NINETEEN
The next generation..208

TE PARAE RECIPES...222

TE PARAE POEMS..246

SELECT BIBLIOGRAPHY..255

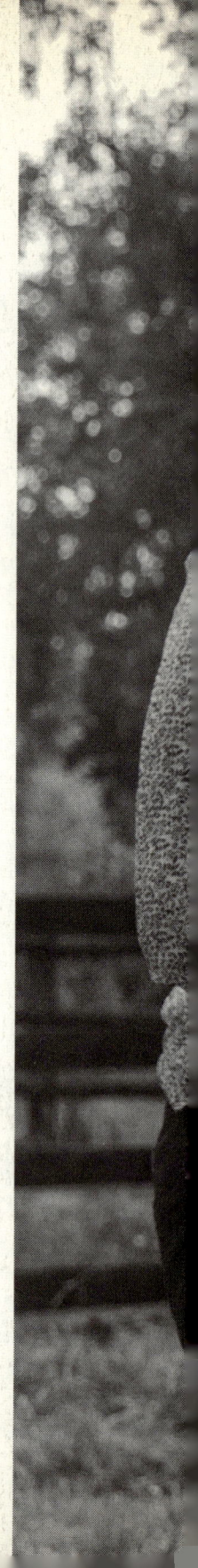

Hine-Waka's favorite spot in the kitchen, in front of the log burner.

CHAPTER ONE

Night sweats

It's the middle of the night and I'm lying awake asking myself – not for the first time – why I gave up a glamorous job in the city to return to the country and start a business. What possessed me to leave behind a world where I was immersed in luxury designer labels, high fashion and cocktail parties for a challenge that would require me to draw on not only my financial resources and my entire life's experience, but those of my husband and family too?

Just when our lives were swinging along so effortlessly. What was I thinking?

From our double bed, I stare through the bifold windows that overlook the huge lake in front of this old family homestead. The moon is reflecting on the water, as it's done for more than 100 years since my great-grandfather and great-grandmother built the house and landscaped the gardens.

I do love this rural lifestyle, but how come, if I'm so tired when I go to bed, I end up wide awake well before dawn? That doesn't seem right. There's always so much to be done here on the farm each day that, come bedtime, I fall between the sheets exhausted. But despite my body being all tuckered out, my brain has other ideas and sometimes, just after midnight, a little voice inside my head will say it's time to wake up.

I'm not always like this: a worry wart. I'm not neurotic. I usually climb into bed and sleep like a baby, waking up ready to tackle the next day head on.

I listen to the night noises for a while. Whoever says the city never sleeps hasn't stayed up all night in the country. At first it seems deathly quiet, but then from a neighbouring farm away in the distance comes the sound of a frustrated bull that won't stop bellowing. Much closer — outside our kitchen door in fact — a couple of possums are hissing at each other in the top of the Wellingtonia tree. One of our Labradors, Mukwa, is barking like a crazy mutt from her kennel below. She wants someone to go out with a gun and shoot the damn pests and she's right, someone should, or those possums will be climbing down the tree and eating the new shoots off the roses. But her barking just makes the possums hiss even more, rarking her up, and on it goes; fat possums versus black dog.

In the willows across the other side of the lake I can hear a morepork hooting. At least the wild cat I've seen lurking around the stables, probably trying to catch a few mice, won't get its mangy claws into the morepork's chicks, but I make a mental note to trap the cat anyway. No feral cats are permitted to survive around here; they devastate the native bird population. We love to keep all the trees around the place filled with birdsong as a backdrop to our day.

Simon Irving, my husband, sleeps on beside me, oblivious to my restlessness and the entertainment carrying on outside. It's almost a full moon, which doesn't help — it illuminates the night so the animals are on high alert. Like a spotlight, it's shining into our bedroom, throwing shadows on the walls and the ceiling, and adding to my worries: will we get by for another 10 years without having to repaint this room?

I cast my mind back to earlier in the evening, before we came to bed. After a day of visitors, phone calls, rushing around feeling like a rat on a treadmill, we slumped down to a cosy dinner at the big wooden table in the kitchen that easily seats 14 people, and was originally used in the farm woolshed for the wool fleeces. We'd been going over the finances, working out how to trim the budget here so more could be spent there; this big old house, Te Parae, might be gorgeous but it sure takes a huge amount of money to keep afloat. The dogs — Mukwa, Boo the rescue Labrador, Harry the retired racing greyhound and Hine-Waka the border collie — had all flopped onto the floor in front of the log burner, jostling for prime position. They were pretending to sleep as they always do in the evening so that they won't get shooed outside — but if one of us raises our voice you can bet a dog will look up, anxious in case they are in trouble and about to be banished.

We'll get there, we always tell ourselves. Things could be worse. As I lie here trying to stop my overactive mind from veering off into negative thoughts, I remind myself we're well on the way now to firmly establishing ourselves as a destination for special events.

I don't have to push as hard as I did when we first came back here five years ago to convince Aucklanders and other city folk that Te Parae has something special to offer for their wedding, corporate getaway or party weekender. I've got several events booked and confirmed for the next season: numerous weddings, some garden tours, retirement village visits and lunches, historic tours, and several other big affairs that will bring in a steady income.

And I mustn't forget about the horses — that is, the thoroughbred yearlings I'm breeding. They're coming on okay for the sales in the New Year, when they should bring in a reasonable income — several thousand dollars at least. Come on, Angela, I tell myself. Remember it was the money from some of your yearlings in the first place that enabled you and Simon to leave the big smoke of Auckland and buy Te Parae from Mum and Dad when they decided to retire and move out.

I feel a bit better for a while, and even start feeling a bit drowsy, but that doesn't last. Did I imagine it, or was that a minor tremor? Jolly earthquakes. They don't frighten me, but the last big one we had here, in 2014, rocked the old house on its foundations; it also left a roadmap of cracks over some of the interior walls where Mum had done extensive renovations back in 1974 when Princess Anne and her then husband Mark Phillips paid an official royal visit to Te Parae, at that time one of New Zealand's leading thoroughbred studs.

Sigh. I don't need any unexpected or unbudgeted expenses, thank you very much, earthquake gods.

I relax again. It was just the wind stirring and rattling a bit of loose corrugated iron on the gables. Another thing to remind Simon to fix — now quite a list for a former police officer who's rapidly learning what it means to live on a rural property. Not that he's totally given up his job of making sure people keep within the law: three years after we moved here, Simon went from being a detective sergeant in the Masterton police force to being a racing investigator, which is basically a policeman at the races — watching out for drugging or corruption at the gallops, the trots and the greyhound races. With a 17-year career as a frontline policeman behind him, Simon doesn't waste time worrying at night. He's very calm and straightforward.

Not like me right now, fretting about the wind getting up and wondering if I put the warm rugs on the older mares and weanling horses. I think back over the day, rehashing my movements step by step. With so many interruptions in a farm day it's hard to keep track of everything that happens. I'll start out with good intentions — a plan — then suddenly the phone rings and it's my cousin Sam Williams, who runs his own thoroughbred stud, Little Avondale (LA), nearby.

'Gidday Mouse,' he says, using the nickname I've had since I was about five. 'Sam here. I've got a bunch of people here from the Thoroughbred Association who want to have a look around Te Parae. I thought I'd bring them over for a bite to eat. Can you rustle something up for us?'

Oh sure, no problem. One pot of soup, one large bacon and egg pie, a gluten-free apple slice and a batch of muffins later, my plans to start stripping the old paint from one of the bathrooms have gone awry. But Te Parae has been welcoming people through its doors for more than 100 years. Who am I to stop the habits of one very long lifetime?

It's a magical lifestyle, but I can't help wondering if it's sensible, throwing the family home open to the public, more so than before, and turning it into somewhere for crowds of people to visit and take photographs to share on social media, as they inevitably do?

I think about the little two-roomed playhouse outside, over by the vege garden. Built with exactly the same materials as the house — white weatherboards, grey corrugated-iron roof, tiny little door with a dear little knocker — it only comes up to my waist now, but as a little girl I spent hours every day playing in there. As the only girl growing up with three brothers I was pretty much a tomboy, but I loved that little hideaway. I only needed to stoop a little to get inside, and, once there, I could chatter away with my favourite toys. My white cane dolls' pram with its rounded hood is still there — the one I used to push my dolls all around the gardens in.

Down by the lake is the boathouse, where my brothers and I would play all summer long; dragging out the canoes and dinghies, and rowing (without lifejackets) to the other side of the lake, where we'd light a campfire, cook our tea, swim and play then come home after dark.

These very private objects and places of my childhood have now been opened up, like the rest of the house, for the public. The rooms where my brothers and I ran around when we were little, playing hide-and-go-seek with mounted wapiti heads staring down at us. There was always somewhere to hide: a cupboard under the stairs, a drawer in an antique dresser, a wardrobe full of musty riding clothes. Am I now cheapening those memories — and the decades of memories from my ancestors haunting the place — by ushering wedding guests into places like the smoking room for whisky and cigars, then charging them for the pleasure?

I banish these negative thoughts from my mind when I picture the faces of the guests who come to Te Parae for the first time and wander around the rooms, drinking in the history of the portraits and the racing awards, taking huge pleasure from being part of their own family's celebrations in our century-old gardens. We're not going to turn Te Parae into the country equivalent of a gated community, with electric alarms, guard dogs (fat chance with our friendly Labradors) and CCTV running day and night. I don't want to lock all this away, out of sight, when I see how much happiness it can bring to people who arrive as strangers, but after a few days, leave as friends.

Then there are the charity events we hold here — I always get a buzz giving back to the community. It's something Mum loved doing at Te Parae; she never charged for her lifetime of hosting and catering, even when she planned, cooked and worked for weeks ahead. I'm happy to carry on a little of her legacy.

My ancestors — starting with the Reverend Henry Williams and his wife Marianne, who landed in the Bay of Islands in 1823, and continuing down through five generations to my parents, Tom and Gay Williams — were all outgoing, hospitable folk, and Simon and I are determined to continue that tradition.

Is that a southerly I can hear coming up? I worry about the large marquee arriving in a couple of days to be erected on the grand lawn. A big blow's not going to make it pleasant for our next bride, who has ordered garlands of wisteria to decorate the entrance to the reception tent; they'll be swept clean across to the other side of the lake. She especially wanted our white wisteria to hold its blooms for her day, so she could have her photographs taken underneath it — but maybe she mentioned having white and purple wisteria in her bridal bouquet? I start thinking I should get up and check my book to ensure I made a note of this — was it pure white she wanted, or white and purple? We have got both planted; purple on the front of the house and white around the back. They're glorious when in full bloom, and the scent is intoxicating. Just thinking of it reminds me of all those midsummer parties we kids had here — out under the stars with parents, littlies, dogs and ponies. So many happy times.

Come to think of it, I'm sure it was white wisteria she wanted, to match the flock of doves she's having released. Did I book some more doves? Last time we ordered doves, we managed to retain only one out of three of them; the others disappeared after the ceremony, even though Simon had built a lovely dovecote. For a while we had just one lonesome dove. I've heard about doves being dyed all sorts of rainbow colours by a Lord Gerald Berners, who owned a magnificent stately home in England called Faringdon House back in the 1930s, but I think we'll keep ours white.

Oh do please stop wandering, mind! Go to sleep.

Enough. Obviously sleep is not heading my way. It's now three am and time for a cup of something hot. I'll get up, go downstairs and make myself something to drink. I slip into the hallway. No need to turn on the lights; if you blindfolded me, bound and gagged me then spun me round and round until I was dizzy, I'd still find my way around this mansion. I crawled these wooden floors, then toddled them on my fat little one-year-old legs when I was learning to walk. I scooted up and down the hallways on my trike, fell down the stairs and bumped my head more times than Mum growled at me for running inside. It's second nature for me to find my way around in the dark, knowing where the squeaky matai floorboards are even though they're covered in carpet, on my way to the warm kitchen.

Dear old Hine-Waka, our old sheepdog, is out like a light in front of the log burner. My heart skips a beat for a minute — is she actually breathing?

'Waka?' I call. No response. I nudge her with my toe; perhaps it's time — she is, believe it or not, about 20 years old (and I'm not talking dog years). She can't last forever. But her chest rises slowly and falls again: she's okay, just sleeping deeply. Waka doesn't have to worry about cashflow, insurance or accounts to pay. Oh, to be a retired sheepdog living out your days in the Te Parae kitchen.

Cupping my hands around a mug of tea, I look through the windows to the tangled undergrowth coming up beneath some of the trees. My great-grandparents, Guy and Eileen Williams, who built Te Parae in 1905 and established these gardens, planted those exotics, but nature's getting a bit out of hand here. Mum and Dad have planted a whole lot of rhododendrons, hydrangeas and camellias lately, which look good when you can see them, but you have to get pretty close to get a good view. I'm thinking I'd like to make a big clearing over on the northwestern side, so we can put in a permanent marquee. That would be a huge plus. Thing is, I need to get Dad up here and pluck up the courage to discuss it with him. I rehearse in my head how this conversation will go. 'So, Dad, here's what I'd like to do over there under those 100-year-old trees: I'd like to take a chainsaw to them.' It's pretty drastic, but Dad's not averse to dramatic change. We'll see how it goes.

I rinse out my cup and up-end it on the draining board, feeling better already. Dad's a good listener. He's been here before — up and down. As have his parents, grandparents. I'm not the first person at Te Parae to worry in the wee hours.

The possums have finished their nonsense discussion and crawled back into their hollow in the Wellingtonia — or scampered down to eat the roses, but I'll deal with that tomorrow. We must have those blooms looking perfect for our summer wedding bookings. Mukwa's stopped her barking too, no doubt circling several times as Labradors do before they settle nose-to-tail and sleep until dawn peeps into their kennels.

I strain to hear any more noises from outside. Nothing. Sometimes the silence just before the dawn is eerie; it can certainly unnerve our city friends when they come to stay, accustomed as they are to sirens, chatter and the stop-start of vehicles outside.

I pad back upstairs to bed, thinking how funny it is that the floorboards never seem to creak on the way back to the bedroom. I'll be weary in the morning, but I'll cope. Must make a big effort not to be grumpy. I slide into bed, trying not to wake up Simon, cuddling into his back.

'Everything okay?' he mumbles sleepily.

'Everything's going to be fine,' I reply, more than a little hopefully.

I guess my ancestors spoke the same way whenever they too got out of bed to talk themselves down from the high branches of self-doubt.

Angela's great grandfather, Guy Williams, sailing his waka in front of a newly built Te Parae homestead, around 1906. The waka is now used as the alter for wedding ceremonies in the garden.

CHAPTER TWO

Reel back the years

Let me take you on a whistle-stop tour through my family history, and explain a bit about why Simon and I decided to leave Auckland and come back to my roots at Te Parae.

On the one hand it was not too difficult to make the break with city life. We'd deliberately not purchased a house in the city because we had always imagined living on a lifestyle block; we often discussed settling somewhere near Christchurch, where Simon hails from. Even though he'd been brought up in suburbia, he'd always worked on farms in the Blenheim area during the summer holidays for the parents of his friend at St Andrew's College, doing everything from milking 200 cows to picking kiwifruit and harvesting garlic. Then, when the land became more valuable for grapes, he helped put in the trellising, put up the wires and later prune the vines.

Yet in other respects we loved our Auckland lifestyle, and we had to think hard about giving it up. We had a pretty carefree, typical DINK (dual income, no kids) routine. We didn't have to plan anything. On a whim we could drive down to Ruapehu on the weekend to go skiing; we'd leave a couple of hours early on Friday afternoon after telling everyone at work, 'Bye, see ya all Monday!' Or we'd scoot up to the Northland beaches in the summer if we felt like it; we'd just water our lemon tree in the pot — the only garden we had — then lock our apartment and go. If we made the decision to move back to the 100-acre Wairarapa farm, which included a 10-acre garden — the section Dad was planning to divide off from the property he'd been farming — well, that would be a totally different situation. We'd be committed seven days a week.

We were very settled in Auckland. Simon had risen to the rank of detective sergeant and he loved his work out in South Auckland. If you asked him to name the highlight of his job he'd never hesitate to answer, 'Serious crime investigation, and in South Auckland we get plenty of that. The homicides, working in a team environment, solving serious crime is the ultimate buzz.'

So for Simon there was considerable sacrifice. He had to factor in that his career advancement would be restricted; in the Counties Manukau area, where he was based, the large number and high turnover of personnel meant that, if you wanted, you could quite rapidly move up the ranks in the force. However, in the Wairarapa, unless he was prepared to work in headquarters in Wellington, he would have to forgo promotion, because he would be moving to work within a much smaller structure in terms of personnel and turnover.

Then again, moving to the Wairarapa would mean enjoying a better lifestyle — Simon acknowledged that, and he'd always enjoyed the country and the quieter regions. After 14 years Auckland was starting to 'grind' with him.

And what did it mean for me — besides giving up wearing designer fashion every day, having manicured nails, attending restaurant openings on Ponsonby Road, and being able to pick and choose whom to admit to the famously fabulous cocktail parties I organised?

I have to admit that I hadn't really anticipated the struggle I would encounter when I left my seven-year position at Louis Vuitton, and exchanged my role as a marketer, events and public relations coordinator for a life back on the farm. I can say I'm thankful to be of tough Williams stock; I come from a long line of bold risk-takers, and even though it's often the Williams men who are talked about, when I look back I think I get a lot of grit from my grandmothers and great-aunts as well.

My great-great-great-grandmother, Marianne Williams, arrived in New Zealand at the age of 29, after a 12-month voyage with her husband and three small children. Her husband, the founder of the Williams family in this country, was the Reverend Henry Williams, who was the leader of the Church Missionary Society in New Zealand in the early nineteenth century and who, among many other accomplishments, translated the Treaty of Waitangi into Maori. They landed on a beach in the Bay of Islands and were immediately surrounded by Maori.

In 1823, Paihia in the Bay of Islands was a settlement with one house — theirs, where the family would live for 30 years. The closest shop was in Sydney, Australia, more than 1800 kilometres away.

Marianne eventually had 11 children. As well as raising her family and supporting her husband, she worked in the community among the Maori as a midwife, nurse and teacher. It would have been a difficult life, but her letters home show how she took this in her stride.

I think of her sometimes and compare her life with my own at Te Parae, with the nearest shop 20 kilometres away in Masterton — and I sometimes think even that is too far when I feel the desperate urge for a latte! When I was in Auckland I could pop around the corner to the nearest café and pick up a coffee; now I have to drive for 30 minutes.

Then there's my great-grandmother Eileen Williams (née Hope-Lewis) who, before she married my great-grandfather Guy, was a champion golfer. She refused to give up her golfing career just because she was helping to build Te Parae, creating the huge gardens, and starting a family. She had won the New Zealand Amateur Match Championship (or Ladies' Open) in 1904 aged 19, and she won it again five more times between 1907 and 1922 (it wasn't held in the war years). She also won provincial championships, travelled overseas to Great Britain and France, then established the New Zealand Ladies' Golf Union. But that's not the half of it. While she was zipping all over New Zealand and overseas, whacking balls around golf courses and winning trophies, she produced four children, one of whom, born in 1908, was my grandfather, Alister Williams. In those days — the early 1900s — it was highly unusual for women to combine family and a sporting career, but from what I've heard passed down through family legend Eileen seemed to cope effortlessly with both. She even became the first woman in New Zealand to obtain her driver's licence.

So when Mum and Dad — Gay and Tom Williams — decided to retire and move out of the homestead I already knew from this family history that there would be very large shoes for me to fill. Initially I didn't think it would be Simon and me who would move in and be responsible for Te Parae — and carry the torch for the next generation. After all, family properties like this, which have been passed down from generation to generation, usually move on to the eldest son; before my twin brother Mark and I were born in 1973, Mum and Dad had already had two sons — Guy in 1970 and Tim in 1971. Both already lived on the Te Parae property; Guy farming and Tim running a helicopter business.

In preparation for moving out of the homestead into a smaller cottage a few kilometres along Te Parae Road, Mum and Dad had been meeting with us kids and discussing their succession plan. Up until now they'd spent their entire marriage — all 48 years of it — farming Te Parae's 809 hectares, and now they had to decide what to do with it.

Top of the list was to sell the lot — homestead and farm; just put it on the open market. Did we want that?

The answer was a unanimous and very loud no! No matter what it took — big mortgages or, as it turned out for Simon and me, sacrificing a successful police career and a glamorous city job — we were determined to keep it in the family.

Obviously Guy, as the eldest, had first choice but he didn't want to move into the big old house; he knew how much money needed to be poured into doing it up and he was totally committed to developing his own farm. Tim was interested but knew he couldn't do the place justice; he thought I was best suited to the house, plus he was focused on his local helicopter business, with all the financial planning that involved.

The main homestead and many of the outbuildings definitely needed a lot of work in terms of repainting. Built of heart native timbers, structurally the house remained strong and sound, but these historic places just eat up money, and it's sometimes years before you see results: bathrooms need renovating, there is heating to be installed, curtains come out second best in the war against destructive ultra-violet rays, and well-worn carpets must be either replaced or covered with designer rugs. Outside there is always painting to be done — bargeboards to be retouched, windowsills to be repainted when the fierce Wairarapa sun has lifted the colour clean off, and don't get me started on the corrugated-iron roof.

Who would be brave enough to take on that kind of financial outlay? And that's before you even start on my dreams for renovating the outlying buildings — the stables, stallion boxes, billiard room, coach houses. And then every day there's the upkeep of the gardens, which includes fencing, lake, lawns, pruning all the trees and taking care of the tennis court. Honestly, it's like buying a museum and then having to find the money to look after all the treasures!

I'm sure there are many families out there who know how difficult family-succession planning can be, particularly when land is involved. It certainly is a credit to my parents that they were able to negotiate and find a solution to suit everyone's skills — that is, all us children — without us falling out over the discussions. It took many meetings to figure out the best solutions not only for the property, but also for the whole family, including Simon.

Simon definitely didn't want to be, as he put it, the 'wanker son-in-law who comes in and takes over the traditional old homestead where older brothers have first right'. So he had a private talk with my brothers before we made any final decisions. They repeatedly reassured Simon they didn't want to take over the homestead and were happy for us to live in it. So it seemed like there were no more excuses holding us back.

Then it came to the crunch. If my two older brothers didn't want it, that left Simon and me. 'Mouse,' said Dad, 'it's over to you. You and Simon can buy the homestead and 100 hectares.' The remaining land, around 709 hectares, would be for Guy (the majority) and Tim.

Before we signed the papers we had to weigh up our options and write down the pros and cons: this was a life-changing decision. Simon does not make snap or irrational decisions; he is very measured. It was part of his job as an investigative police officer to consider all the factors, what courses of action you could take and then choose the right one.

I knew this wasn't the first time the Te Parae property had been split up. Back in my great-great-grandfather Thomas Coldham Williams's day (he was known to all as TC Williams), Te Parae had once been part of a huge tract of land in conjunction with the Beethams of Brancepeth. But I've heard it said before that we can't look to the future without looking at the past. If it suited old TC when he had to split up the family land, I could make it work out for me, couldn't I?

The magnificent Brancepeth Station homestead.

Angela's great grandfather, Guy Coldham Williams.

CHAPTER THREE

Nothing new under the Te Parae sun

The main difference when the Te Parae land was split up back in the days of TC Williams (who was born in 1825) was that he came to the Wairarapa with enough resources to hire plenty of men and women to help on the property — not that he and his family didn't work just as hard as Simon and I do.

Trouble is that Simon and I would have to do all the hard labour ourselves (apart from roping in Mum, Dad and extended family on no wages). Unlike the days of TC, when there was no minimum wage, we couldn't afford to hire screeds of workers to cut down trees, paint sheds, clear out rubbish and do the gardens.

Why did TC come to the Wairarapa, when he was born in the Bay of Islands? Well, he ended up in Masterton because he had married Annie Beetham. The Beetham family were the original founders of this community. Annie's parents, William and Mary, arrived in Wellington in 1855 and lived in the Hutt Valley in a house called Te

Mako. But, even before they left Surrey in England, they had their sights on purchasing and farming land in the Wairarapa, despite the fact that they had come from a small landholding, and that William was a professional portrait painter.

William Beetham would have struggled initially to support his family. There would have been savings, and his eldest son Richmond (Dick), an engineer, had already left England in 1853 and gone to Australia to seek his fortune. The other children were William Junior, Anne, George, Hugh, Charles, Mary-Margaret, Susan, Phillip and Norman. Richmond soon joined his family in New Zealand and found work supervising the finishing of the road over the summit of the Rimutaka Hill.

But how do the Williamses fit into all this?

Like other Christian settlers, the Beethams worshipped at Christ Church in Taita, which was built the year before they arrived and is still standing; it's the oldest church in the Wellington region. Reverend Thomas Hutton's wife, Sarah, was the sister of TC Williams, and the Hutton, Beetham and Williams families all socialised together. TC became friendly with Annie Beetham, and they eventually married.

Within a few years, William and Mary had saved enough money from Richmond's Rimutaka job to put with their savings and lease a sheep-and-cattle station in the Wairarapa. Negotiations began between William Junior and George and their then friend Jack Hutton (a relative of Reverend Hutton) to purchase the lease of 10,000 acres of challenging country at Wainuioru, east of Masterton, which they called Brancepeth — including what is now Te Parae.

But after a short time, for reasons that are unclear, Jack Hutton left the partnership and found his way to the South Island goldfields. Richmond and Hugh then took the lease from Jack Hutton and from 1875 the four Beetham brothers leased the Brancepeth land from the government. The original Brancepeth station (encompassing the Te Parae land) was wild, untamed swamp and bush with large areas of native grass. This was known as the pastoral era of the 1850s and 1860s: it was no use buying or leasing blocks of land smaller than 10,000 acres, as anything smaller wasn't financially viable.

William and Mary Beetham never fully settled at Brancepeth, staying only nine months, but it must have been a huge culture shock. In Upper Hutt, they grew potatoes and did odd jobs around the neighbourhood. Over the Rimutaka Hill on their new wilderness block, everything changed. There was no such thing as making do with the small-scale plots they'd been accustomed to back in England's green and pleasant land. The New Zealand countryside had to be cleared of massive trees, using hand-held pitsaws, swamps had to be drained, and huge logs hauled away by bullock teams. Progress was slow, so the amount of productive land was precious. Stock could only be purchased as land was cleared, and income was meagre.

Back at the end of the nineteenth century, even though at 31,000 hectares Brancepeth was the largest sheep station in the Wairarapa, the Beethams were beaten back by rabbits, bad weather, bush clearing and, most of all, debt. To put it bluntly, they were financially unable to freehold the property. Their father saw the way forward with TC Williams: if they formed a partnership with TC, he figured their problems would be reduced — not solved, as problems never are in farming — but at least they could freehold the land. So that's what happened.

Not that it was easy after an injection of capital. The days of shipping frozen lamb from Dunedin to Britain were still two decades away, so there was no great market for lamb or mutton, except for home kill or local sales. Sheep were really only farmed for their wool, and when they reached the age of about five they were culled.

TC Williams had foresight, though, and opened up a factory at Waingawa, where Borthwicks later set up their freezing works. Here sheep carcasses were rendered down to make tallow to be exported.

***

The Beethams built a 32-room, 10,000-square-foot homestead, still known today as the Brancepeth homestead and registered with Heritage New Zealand as a Category One property (the highest rating). It was substantially rebuilt in 1905, replacing the original 1858 homestead, but the original woolshed, slaughterhouse and other outbuildings remain preserved just as they were back in those struggling days of the nineteenth century.

I have fond memories of Brancepeth when I was little. It's only about five minutes' drive from Te Parae. We used to go there for drinks at Easter and Christmas, when Dad's godfather, Hugh, and his wife, Barbara, (known as Snooks) were living there. Mum and Dad and the other adults would settle down with their long gins, and all us kids would be left to our own devices.

I have magical recollections of running riot inside the amazing two-storey mansion with a third level that could only be accessed by secret stairs built into the ceiling — up and down the main staircase and the servants' one, all along the corridors — while the parents ignored us; we were out of sight, out of mind. Outside there was a massive in-ground concrete swimming pool — well, as a little kid, I thought it was massive — and then there were all the outbuildings to explore, including the beautiful old stables. I remember they had special partitions that were cleverly designed with guttering along the floor so they could be hosed out, making it easier for the stablehands.

It really was — and still is — such a beautiful old place. All the historic furniture and knick-knacks, the crockery and the silver are still there. And the library: there's a great story about one of the old sofas in the library, where an old local Maori chief, Piripiri, would come to sit and rest. Hugh, fluent in Maori, and Piripiri would sit for hours in the library chatting. Piripiri would never sleep upstairs in the homestead, always on his sofa (which was the first piece of furniture made by the Beetham brothers for the homestead and is still in the same spot in the library today). There was the odd occasion where Hugh would find Piripiri asleep on the floor in front of the fire the following morning.

Today Te Parae is still linked with Brancepeth because together we host historic tours. A busload will go around Brancepeth in the morning, where Edward Beetham explains a brief history of Brancepeth and the Beetham family, then the tours come on here to Te Parae, where they get the story of our place, how the families and properties are connected, and stay for lunch.

***

By all accounts, my great-great-grandfather TC Williams was an impressive figure. Premier William Fox described him as 'six feet odd without his shoes; in robust health and the full vigour of mature age; strong enough to grapple, not only with the case before the Court, but with the biggest member of the sixteen tribes'. There were few people, apparently, who tangled with him — not even the local publican, who was rumoured to have shortchanged TC's fencers when they put their pay-cheques on the bar. A few hundred pounds would normally do for several weeks' beers, but word got back from the Taueru Pub when the lads returned earlier than usual, ready for work and needing more money. TC was having none of this. He saddled up, rode out to the Taueru Pub and demanded a refund. The denials and blustering were brushed aside; TC calmly took out his revolver, aimed it at the top shelf and blew out the line of bottles behind the bar. The barman quickly paid up before he was shot, too.

I'm sure this is true; and, anyway, I'm told there were bullet holes behind the bar when they pulled the pub down some years later.

But pressures like rabbits, disease and government tax policies of dividing up big-run holdings didn't really cause the breakup of the Williams–Beetham partnership. There were many other reasons, not least the fact that the original Beetham offspring of William and Mary had married and by now had children who also wanted to go farming in their own right. In a move that would in some ways foreshadow my own parents' succession plan at Te Parae, on 31 July 1903 the Beetham–Williams partnership was formally dissolved — or at least the dissolution began, and two years later the partition of lands was amicably completed.

Which brings this pocket-sized history to the building of Te Parae homestead in 1905, when TC Williams was recorded as the original owner, with 5000 acres of land, 23,248 sheep and 1435 cattle. Scrupulous in his endeavours to be fair, he even listed and divided everything down to minutiae such as '1 painkiller, 1 set dog cart harness, 1 bone crusher, ½ case vinegar'. I'm pleased my parents weren't that meticulous in listing every single chattel in the place, though I'm sure if you fossick around in the stables or the cupboards upstairs at Te Parae today you'll probably discover that half case of vinegar or that bone crusher — such is our family's compulsion for hoarding.

Another generational difference in attitudes is that, although immediately after 1905 TC set out on paper the division of the Te Parae property among his 13 children (this was when Guy inherited Te Parae homestead), he directed that they were not to receive their share until the boys — Hugh, Guy, Wyvern, Algar and Erl — were aged 21 and the girls — Ethel, Maude, Hilda, Elfie, Gwynne, Ila, Elva and Githa — were 25. One of his sons, Wyvern, was so upset when he was later cut out of his inheritance for arguing with TC that he died of ill health shortly afterwards, aged 39.

My parents were much more liberal: they have helped us all the way, no matter our age; and there's no way they would dictate that I would have to wait until I was 25 to inherit, just because I'm a girl!

TC and Annie lived out the rest of their lives in Wellington, in an imposing two-storeyed mansion on Hobson Street. A photograph shows double columns on the front veranda, a balcony above, then a square, flat-roofed tower. A fernery to the side, opposite a large bay window, completes a scene like something out of a Katherine Mansfield short story. But TC still ruled with an iron fist, dictating that, if any of his sons were 'by reason of immoral or drunken habits or a spendthrift disposition or otherwise unfitted to be entrusted with uncontrolled property', the trustees could withhold the inheritance.

***

Now, up in Auckland, Simon and I had in front of us the papers that would enable us to purchase the family homestead and keep it in the Williams family for the next generation. Should we take the plunge and sign, or should we stay in our comfort zone?

The gates of Te Parae, covered in snow.

Mares and foals grazing at Te Parae.

CHAPTER FOUR

Thoroughbred stud once more?

I decided the final call had to be Simon's; after all, he was the one who was sacrificing his opportunity for promotion and having to apply for a transfer to the Masterton police. Also he had to think about where he was heading; I was not going to force my husband's hand when it came to moving into my family home, the place I was brought up in.

But that wasn't the only issue. Te Parae, like all old wooden buildings that have fallen well down the list of priorities of a demanding farming business, needed a huge amount of money spent on it. Leaving Auckland and my job would mean giving up our double income and greatly increasing our expenditure. We had to face up to the fact that our new life would undoubtedly be a financial struggle. Living half an hour out of Masterton would not offer hoards of clients beating down our door if we decided to run a bed and breakfast, homestay or farmstay like some rural people choose to operate out of their family homesteads.

Perhaps I could take Te Parae back to being a top thoroughbred-breeding stud again? I thought about that. Maybe I could get Uncle Buzz, Dad's brother, to help. He had been there when Te Parae had been one of the leading thoroughbred studs in the country; he certainly knew his stuff, and Dad would lend a hand. I already had the mares grazing away in the paddocks, well settled in, and I wouldn't be the first woman to take the reins at Te Parae in terms of turning out fine horses for the yearling sales and racetrack; when Guy Williams retired from Te Parae, his son Alister (Dad's father) took over and the place headed in a slightly different agricultural direction, and it was a woman who took it there. In those years Te Parae went from being a sheep-and-cattle station to one of New Zealand's best-known thoroughbred horse studs. It is also known as one of the oldest studs in New Zealand, so I wondered if maybe that reputation deserved to be restored and continued.

Today, visitors to Te Parae will often do a double-take when they stroll around the side of the homestead, admiring the waist-high vegetable gardens Mum and Dad created in large old concrete water troughs, then catching sight of what looks like eight gravestones under the soaring Wellingtonia tree. These are, in fact, granite memorials in honour of Te Parae's finest thoroughbreds: three stallions, Sabean, Agricola and Oncidium, and four mares, Sunbride, Lowland, Impeccable and Dicidiana. The eighth tablet commemorates my grandfather Alister, who presided over the stud in its heyday, and died when he was 63 years old. As visitors read the inscriptions they'll probably be joined by my cheeky chooks, Red Shavers who have no respect for history but will peck at visitors' shoes or forage for something nice to eat among the memorials to those who put this place on the map.

What the visitors won't realise is that it was not actually Alister but his wife Nancy who was responsible for Te Parae shooting from being just another big New Zealand sheep-and-cattle station to one of the country's top thoroughbred horse studs. Today there is still a fair amount of discrimination against women in the racing industry, no doubt about that; but Nancy, or Granny Andy as she was known to us, was a real trail-blazer. And there was absolutely no way Granny Andy would let any man push her around or tell her what to do — least of all her husband, Alister. She sold the first yearling for $100,000.

So it occurred to me, when I thought about what we could do to generate enough income to support the upkeep of the homestead, that perhaps I could take a leaf out of her book and build up a stud of my own? Could it be possible to take Te Parae back to the heights of the thoroughbred-breeding industry as it was in my grandparents' day, when leading buyers and trainers, including the likes of the late and great Bart Cummings, came from all over the world to view their sires and yearlings?

***

Before Granny Andy married, she was Nancy Teschemaker, from the Waihopai Valley in Marlborough, with a solid reputation as a competitive horsewoman at Agricultural and Pastoral (A&P) shows and jumping events. She had met my grandfather on a family outing at the Trentham races and they'd become engaged three days later. As she was preparing to move north to Te Parae, arranging to bring her team of working dogs and horses (broodmares) with her, my grandfather realised his new bride would be bringing horses that he believed were of no use for rounding up sheep and cattle. To him, broodmares were a frivolous hobby. He was happy for the dogs to come — after all, they'd be helpful on the farm — but broodmares, he said, were no use at all. She could leave them behind.

'No broodmares,' she retorted, 'no Nancy.'

Alister quickly changed tack at the prospect of losing his bride; perhaps broodmares might not be such a bad idea after all. So Nancy moved into Te Parae, and her two mares — one she'd bought for five pounds, the other she'd been given because it was deemed incapable of breeding — moved into the paddocks.

Nancy had already proved herself to be no mere dilettante: with her horses and team of dogs, she had worked on other farms around Marlborough during the Depression, bringing in much-needed cash to assist the family finances during lean times. And, not only was she a good worker and rider, but she was also great at working with horses. Both mares she brought up with her from the South Island produced good foals, and just three years after she married, Te Parae's first colt, by Valkyrian out of Auspicious, sold at Trentham.

My grandfather, a big, staunch man, never regretted changing his mind about having broodmares on the property. He very quickly became fascinated by the art of breeding thoroughbreds. He cultivated an interest in bloodstock pedigrees, and soon became quite an expert. He was a co-founder of the Thoroughbred Breeders Association and earned a reputation as one of the most discerning and successful breeders of the post-war era.

In 1941, when Alister and Nancy sold their first yearling from Te Parae, the yearling sales were held at Trentham Racecourse near Wellington. The first national sales were held there in 1927. The following year a big colt nobody thought would amount to anything sold for £168 to an Australian buyer. That horse was Phar Lap. Every buyer goes to the sales dreaming of finding a Phar Lap, and every breeder, if they're like me, aims to come up with a Group One winner, the holy grail — a horse that wins, for example, the Melbourne Cup.

My grandfather was obviously quite the man. Born and brought up in provincial Wairarapa, he left Wanganui Collegiate with a distinguished reputation as both a scholar and sportsman — a rower, captain of the 1926 First XV and an athletics champion. He then went to England to attend Jesus College, Cambridge University. Upstairs at Te Parae, on top of one of the high shelves, I found an old woven-leather suitcase — a real collectible — with a luggage tag dating back to the 1930s, upon which is printed 'New Zealand Railways' and, in cursive writing, 'A. C. Williams'. I am sure this is the suitcase my grandfather took with him to Cambridge.

Unlike his father, Guy — a stern disciplinarian who once banned Alister from having any more dances at Te Parae because he had livened things up by ordering a beer keg — Alister was amiable and loved socialising with and working alongside the men on the farm. When he and Nancy married in Blenheim, the newspapers wrote it up in detail with descriptions of her wedding gown and those of the bridesmaids and the mother-of-the-bride, and even the cake decorations — right down to the silver horses and horseshoes that Nancy had ordered to be placed all around the sides of the white icing.

Under Alister and Nancy's ownership, Te Parae quickly became the leading stud in the Wairarapa, up there with New Zealand's best. Its first sire was Sabean, bought for 2000 guineas, who produced offspring that grossed over $1 million. Next came Agricola, the first syndicated stallion to come to New Zealand, then Oncidium, another sire whose tablet sits under the Wellingtonia tree. Many racing and thoroughbred writers praised Oncidium, not just in terms of his prowess, but in language that went over the top in emotional terms.

For example, British journalist Andrew Pelis, looking back in 2014 on the 'greats' of racing, said he had actually 'fallen in love' with Oncidium and 'became hooked on racing' because of him — the horse was the first winner he had ever backed. That was in 1965, at the Coronation Cup. But Oncidium was extraordinary. He had topped the Australian and New Zealand sires list three times and produced a legendary roll of honour including Leilani (Caulfield Cup), Taras Bulba (AJC Derby), Dayana (VRC Derby, AJC Derby, West Australian Derby, Australian Derby), Gold Brick (AJC Derby), Young Ida (NZ Oaks), Sandarae (VRC Oaks), Grand Cidium (Caulfield Guineas) and Oncidon (Metropolitan Handicap). He was also a champion broodmare sire in New Zealand.

Every January, before the Trentham sales, the yearlings would be groomed and polished, so they shone like the family silver, then paraded around the lawn, under the oak and weeping elm trees, before an admiring crowd. As more horses were added to the stud, and because visitors wanted to wander around inspecting the property, the stables needed to be expanded and gussied up. They added more horseboxes behind the 14 timber originals, and horse yards spreading down under the trees.

I look back and am so proud of the reputation my grandparents built up. It can't have been easy — especially for Nancy, being a woman in a man's world in those days — but they obviously had a gift for it, because the champions kept on coming. Straight Draw, a yearling out of Te Parae mare Sunbride (also memorialised under the tree) won the Melbourne Cup in 1957. Dayana, who won not only the Victoria Racing Club Derby but a record four derbies in Australia in one year, was by Oncidium out of Dicidiana. Nancy bought Sunbride because she liked her classic head, and she foaled a famous racehorse called Ilumquh, who won the Caulfield Cup in 1960 and was a place-getter in the 1960 and 1963 Melbourne Cup.

My grandmother deserves enormous credit not just for founding Te Parae Stud in the face of her new husband's doubts, and not just for her success as a thoroughbred breeder, but also for having something more: a special eye for picking greatness in a horse and then the patience to wait for that horse's talents to emerge. Where others might have given up too early, sold the horse, then regretted it when they saw another breeder reaping the rewards, Granny Andy refused to take advice if it went against her instincts — even if that advice came from her own husband.

Sunbride, for instance — that wonderful mare — didn't start off so well. Her first four progeny, all fillies, didn't shine when they went to the track, and when she was in foal the fifth time to Faux Tirage my grandfather thought it was time to give up. 'This mare Sunbride's no good,' he told Nancy. 'I think you should sell her.'

But Nancy was having none of that. 'I refuse to entertain any thought of selling Sunbride,' she told a reporter when asked if the mare was for sale. 'When I go broke and I am evicted from Te Parae, Sunbride and I will walk down the road together.'

That fifth foal was the aforementioned Straight Draw, which won the 1957 Melbourne Cup, Sydney Cup and AJC Metropolitan.

Was I dreaming? For me to acquire a stallion in 2011 anywhere near the standard of Oncidium with our meagre finances, when the homestead was demanding so much attention, would be foolish to say the least; even to syndicate such a sire takes a huge amount of hard work and dedication. But, if I couldn't stand a stallion here, what else did I have at Te Parae to build on if I was to become the next Nancy Williams?

Angela's grandparents, Alister and Nancy Williams, with Ilumquh and his trainer, Eric Ropiha and exercise rider, Vern Baley.

Angela with her first pony, Handy Andy.

CHAPTER FIVE

Horses, my passion

Like many girls of my era who grew up on a farm in New Zealand, my real passion was horses. I was so lucky — the envy, I guess, of every city kid who begs her parents for a pony, reads all the horsey adventure books she can get her hands on, and saves her pocket money for riding lessons on the outskirts of town.

All I had to do was walk out the back door, push my feet into jodhpur boots, whistle for the Labradors, catch my horses, saddle them up in our lovely old stables and go for a trot around the property that Dad was farming in those days. All seven of us — counting my cousins who grew up on the same farm and lived a couple of kilometres up the road at Ngaipo — learned to ride. My cousin Anna Williams and I remained horse mad, whereas the boys soon found that motorbikes go faster and are far less temperamental.

In the winter school holidays, there was hunting: galloping

across the farmland following the master, who in turn followed the huntsman and the whips, who were in charge of the hounds. The hounds chased a hare, which always went in a wide circle and was seldom caught because it could dash through fences faster than the hounds. We had to jump the fences — either full wire or spars, where the top wire is lowered and a wooden pole is attached to the next wire. It was enormous fun. We often took risks and fell off, but hardly ever got hurt.

During the summer months we would travel throughout the Wairarapa entering as many pony classes as we could at the gymkhanas, country sports days and the local A&P shows, from the show ring classes to dressage, show jumping and jumping cross country.

Even when I was living and working in Auckland after I came back from London and Scotland, I somehow organised things so I could keep working with horses. I kept a couple of thoroughbred broodmares back at Te Parae, farming them with Dad, who was my sixty-something stablehand. I'm sure Dad used to shudder when I phoned after the mares' sales at Karaka, in South Auckland: 'Dad, a Majestic horse float will be coming up the drive in the next few days. There will be a couple of mares — can you please unload them and pop them into the paddock? I bought them at the sales.'

WaitAMinute was my first broodmare. She arrived 16 years ago as a gift from Dad and she's still out in the paddock, producing foals, although Dad likes to teasingly remind me that I owe him for her! They say horses are in your blood, but I learned quite a lot of what I know about breeding horses in my childhood by observing what goes on here at Te Parae.

As kids we rarely had summer holidays, because that was the busiest time of the year here, when the yearlings were in the stables. Grooms would come from all over New Zealand, and some from

Australia and England, to work here and prepare the young horses for the sales. For as long as I can remember, straight after breakfast I would wander over to the stables and hang around these horse people all day. I'd sit in the hay manger and watch what was going on. My brother Mark, already an entrepreneur at an early age, would spend the morning making banana fritters, then take them over to the stables and sell them for a dollar apiece to the staff at morning tea. They would lap them up. It didn't take me long to jump on the bandwagon so I could get a cut of the action.

As children we would disappear for hours, following the grooms around, watching them prepare their allocated yearlings — feeding the young horses, grooming them, walking them. We would often go back to the workers' cottage and have lunch, then spend the afternoon around the broodmares, which were located across the lake. It would be getting on to dusk by the time we made our way back home.

To this day I still run into people who worked at Te Parae when I was a kid, and without fail they tell me stories of their time here. Most of them have remained friends with our family, wherever they have ended up in the world. Neill Ross was one of our grooms in the mid 1980s. One of his jobs was to look after former champion Straight Draw when he was retired and over 20 years old. Straight Draw was blind and deaf by this stage, but Neill remembers taking his hot feed to the top of the paddock: 'I never worked out how he knew his feed or I were there, but he used to bolt from the far end of the paddock at a rapid clip, slam on the anchors and slide up right in front of the feed bin and hammer down his food.'

Neill was a teenager when he lived at Te Parae; it was his first job out of school. He stayed with us for two and a half years, and was treated like family even when there wasn't work to be done — 'Like the time, for your mother's birthday, when all the guests paddled across the lake and dressed up as pirates and we attacked them with water bombs.'

Dad taught us to ride in his inimitable way. He put Mark and me up on a big old thoroughbred mare when we were about two years old — no bridle, no halter, nothing, just two little pipsqueaks on top together. I didn't get my first pony until I was about six. His name was Handy Andy and he was, I have to say, a wee devil. He used to dump me left, right and centre, then take off and run to the other end of the paddock, trying not to be seen for the rest of the day. I would stumble home crying and Mum or Dad would have to catch him again, but it taught me good balance. I soon learned when he was about to buck and I'd hold on tight, so the dumpings became less frequent. He was about 12 hands high (a hand is four inches, or around 10 centimetres). I soon moved on to a big — well, big for an eight-year-old — 14-hand pony called Tuppence, a pretty grey mare that was three-quarter Arab so also had the potential to throw a wobbly. I'd go to pony club at Mamaku or Morland which coincidentally were both part of the original Brancepeth station, just down the road, and every day my cousin Anna and I would spend hours together on our ponies.

I then moved on to a lovely roan-coloured pony called Sandy. She would jump anything — full wire fences, brush jumps, water jumps. We had a lot of fun at the shows and gymkhanas around the Wairarapa. My final pony was a big, solid 14.2-hand gelding called Tiranui Shar. This was when I was in boarding school at Woodford House in Havelock North, so I couldn't ride every day.

During my time at Wainuioru Primary School, then at Hadlow Preparatory and later St Matthew's Collegiate (both in Masterton) my cousin Anna and I would come home, get off the school bus and race to see who could catch their pony and saddle up the fastest. We would arrange a special meeting point to catch up then we'd ride around the farm, up to the big tank stands, or gallop along the airstrip paddock. In the weekends we would take the ponies to the Wainuioru River down by the Brancepeth Bridge for a swim. They were such good times. Mum and Dad would cart me off to the Langdale, Tinui and Gladstone horse sports days, where I'd win the odd ribbon to decorate my bedroom wall. It was an idyllic childhood, and horses really were my life. Growing up on a farm, I never had to worry about where to ride or where to graze them.

It was very picturesque, too — and still is. That would be another drawcard for visitors to the renewed stud: seeing the restored stables and outbuildings, which had been added to when Nancy and Alister first grew the reputation of the place.

Sometime after the Te Parae homestead was built, a pit-sawn native-timber building for storing grain and feed was erected across the way from the main house. It had a large loft upstairs, complete with upstairs doorway and hook for hoisting heavy loads aloft, and chutes for delivering the grain to those waiting below. At one time it would have been capable of holding massive amounts of feed. There were several loose boxes below, where the horses were brought in to be groomed and inspected. The farrier would have been a familiar sight, unloading his brazier in the yard, pulling on his leather apron, hammering the shoes to fit horses for work on the hills or pulling buggies along the stony roads into town.

In other parts of the building, where the steep pitch of the roof sloped down, carriages, buggies and harness were stored — cobblestones below, cobwebs above. Back before the motorcar took over, the carriages would go in and out every day with horses backed into them. If you wander around this area today, nearly a hundred years later, not a lot has changed. You could close your eyes and imagine the scene — farrier shoeing a horse over there, the sound of hooves striking the cobbles as another carriage horse trots out into the drive, the occasional curse from a strapper inside a loose box, and no doubt the clucking of chooks pecking around for fallen oats from the mouths of mares munching their daily tucker.

But could I produce horses that would come up to the standards of Granny Andy, Alister, Dad and Uncle Buzz? When I look back at the quality of the bloodstock that have gone down the drive and out of the gates of Te Parae, it scares me more than a little. As anyone who keeps horses knows, having these beasties is a huge responsibility; they take up quite a chunk of your day every day — and for what kind of financial return? I could forget about this aspect when I was living the glam life in Auckland and letting Dad sweat the dirty work, even in foul weather when he had to pull on wet-weather gear and Red Bands and do the feeding-out. When I was home at the weekend I got sharp reminders of what it was like. If it had been raining for days, we'd be rocking and rolling down the tracks on the quadbike, through knee-high mud. My horses would be happy to see me with a load of hay and hard feed, and the naughty boys might chew through the bungee cords in their eagerness to pinch it all. Male horses are such troublemakers — that's why I try to stick to females. It's not always easy, though: even when I was coming home just for a weekend, someone would ring to ask me to take in a horse they couldn't handle. And if I did agree to do it I'd only get paid grazing money; I wouldn't get a wage or an hourly rate for training or handling the horse. For example, if I took in a rising two-year-old colt that was tiny, naughty and wouldn't do what he was told — not evil, just never properly trained — that would take up two hours of my day, every day, by the time I caught him, calmed him, trained him to headstall, rugged him then turned him out again.

I've had all sorts of phone calls from people wanting me to help pultice ponies' hooves to help draw out infections from the wet weather, or remove the stitches from a wound that has healed. It helps that I was a vet nurse in Carterton for two years, employed by South Wairarapa Vets, before I moved to Auckland. I saw pretty much everything there: castrating cats, comforting old grannies whose dearly loved moggies died under the anaesthetic — that wasn't good — and cutting abscesses out of dogs' teeth. When you pop an abscess that has closed over and filled with pus, it lets out the most terrible smell that really turns your stomach.

The thing I found hardest to take in that job, though, was when people came in and asked us to put down their pets just because they couldn't be bothered looking after them any more. Often the animal would be perfectly healthy, and still in the puppy or kitten stage. It really annoyed me. I felt like asking them why they didn't think more carefully about getting a pet in the first place. I wouldn't say anything — I was professional, and couldn't berate customers — but I found it hard to cope with. I didn't cry, but I would have a heavy heart for a while.

I'm not one to show my emotions, and that goes for the way I behave around my horses, too. I'm not one for high drama or big displays of affection, throwing my arms around their necks, or anything I consider OTT. It's just not me.

***

I was back to wondering if I could really make a viable business out of recreating Te Parae as a leading thoroughbred-breeding centre. Despite all my background and experience I had to face facts: it didn't make sense to try to make just over 100 acres — with 10 acres of gardens — into a financially successful horse stud. For one thing, that's not the way thoroughbred breeding is heading these days. I could try, but it would be a struggle because, in the breeding world, it's the biggest studs that come out on top while the smaller studs and the small-time breeders are being whittled away. The industry is carried by a dozen or so large studs, and the future does not bode well for small-time breeders. I can't see a place for Te Parae as a stud in today's world of horse breeding.

Also, there was my cousin Sam a few kilometres away at Little Avondale, already a highly successful stud; I could jump on his coat-tails. Why did I need to have a place of my own when I could rely on him? If I could support Sam by agisting for him (taking horses for grazing in return for a fee) throughout the winter, that would work really well. I could raise my yearlings here, prep them for the sales at Karaka in January, then send them to Sam one week before they would go up to Auckland. This would be a far more sensible solution. We could support each other, as opposed to competing.

In reality I knew it was the stuff of dreams, trying to replicate what Nancy and Alister had done — dreams and memories — and I still had plenty of treasures to remind me of what they had achieved.

For instance, one of Granny Andy and Alister's promotional products was a white linen teatowel featuring the names of the horses of Te Parae and the cups they won. I recently found a bundle of them that had never reached the market so I've had them framed and they now take pride of place on the walls in the homestead. The smoking-room walls are lined with paintings of Te Parae's award-winning stallions, and there are trophies and silver cups, including the 1960 Caulfield Cup, scattered around in all the rooms.

Then there are the tales told at family gatherings about the legendary personalities who visited during Te Parae's heyday, such as the aforementioned Bart Cummings, Australia's 'King of Cups', who passed away in September 2015. After Alister and Granny Andy retired, Bart continued coming over the Tasman, and often stayed at Te Parae to see the horses and catch up with Mum, Dad, Buzz and his wife, Susie. One story involved Bart's visit coinciding with a visit from Andrew Peacock, a former leader of the Australian Liberal Party. Dad suggested they see an Oncidium filly owned by a local farmer, Ian McRae. Andrew purchased the filly and Bart trained her; a happy outcome! They were even happier when that filly, Leilani, won a total of six Group One races (the crème de la crème class), including the Caulfield Cup in 1974, and went on to be the Australian Champion Racehorse of 1975.

This of course all happened before my time, or at least when I was a toddler, and these people wouldn't have even noticed me. But I did get to meet Bart Cummings once at the yearling sales when I was in my mid thirties and, hoping for some quick inside advice on how to rear a champion, I told him I came from Te Parae. If I thought that name-dropping would elicit free advice from one of the greats, I was hugely mistaken. In the dry manner for which he was famous, the great trainer looked at me and said, 'Yes, I remember Te Parae. I had very good duck à l'orange there once.'

I scurried away feeling very, very small.

Still, it was a bit of a wrench giving up the decision to honour the Te Parae horse-stud history. When I told people we were leaving Auckland and going back to the Wairarapa to take over the homestead, a few said, 'Te Parae goes with horses. You can't possibly not have horses.'

But that would not have been practical. I really enjoy working with horses — it's my passion — but I had to face the truth: they would not be my mainstay. I could keep them on, but they would have to be secondary to some other source of income. Something more upmarket, I realised, than mucking out stables, brushing manes and tails, feeding out from a quadbike, and taking a gamble on the fertility of broodmares. Something that reflected the glamour and hospitality of my family's past work.

Straight Draw, winner of the 1957 Melbourne Cup. This photo was taken in 1985, when he was 32 years old. He lived to be 35.

Royal visit, 1973. From left to right: Princess Anne, Buzz Williams, Captain Mark Philips, Tom Williams.

CHAPTER SIX

Let us entertain you

If I wasn't to be stud manager at one of the country's top thoroughbred horse studs, then what would the future for Te Parae be? I reflected on another solid reputation my family had established for themselves: throughout the Wairarapa and beyond, Te Parae was renowned as *the* place to go for a great time.

O ver the years — decades, in fact — the Williamses had made a name for themselves as terrific hosts, great at entertaining people from all walks of life. They included everyone in the fun — staff, dignitaries, all were welcome. And not only here at Te Parae were the Williamses renowned for splendid parties and dinners, but they were also known for kick-starting events like Wings Over Wairarapa, which now draws enormous crowds and famous people such as movie directors Sir Peter Jackson and James Cameron.

These Williams parties were nothing new. Society pages in

archived newspapers reported every social gathering, every glittering occasion, be it a ladies' high tea or the annual ball, and described them down to the last sparkling jewel worn by each woman. The Williamses and Beethams had obviously made it socially, because they featured regularly.

The lifestyle at large, bustling stations like Te Parae and Brancepeth must have seemed fabulous from the outside. There were servants, horse-drawn buggies with footmen in blue uniforms, candlelit dinners and balls. The dinner tables were laid with the finest crystal. And because the Williamses socialised with the Beethams, who had their own vineyards, they could offer their guests their fine wines. Brancepeth, too, boasted a library with some 2000 books.

After TC and Annie retired to live in Hobson Street in Wellington, they held huge parties there that often featured in the Wellington papers. They even had minor royalty staying with them — the Countess of Glasgow, Lady Augusta, Lady Alice and Lady Dorothy Boyle, who all, according to the *Press* of Christchurch, 'passed through . . . accompanied by Captain Campbell-Preston. For one night they were the guests of Miss Williams, during the absence of Mrs T. C. Williams in Christchurch.'

It's easy to imagine the excitement and buzz when, in February 1909, TC's wife, Annie, held a party at Hobson Street that was so gushingly written about by the *Evening Post* that it's worth quoting in full:

> There is no house in Wellington better suited for entertaining purposes than that of Mr T. C. Williams in Hobson Street, and last night all the rooms and the large hall that is such a feature of the residence were filled with gaily frocked guests. The occasion was a farewell to Miss Una [Elva] and Miss Eila Williams [daughters of TC and Annie], whose coming marriages are to take place in Auckland.

The night was perfect, and the open doors and windows prevented the heat being oppressive. The flowers were lovely. On every vantage-point in the drawing-rooms were arranged sweet peas — masses of delicate or vivid colour. Flowering pot plants and palms, too, were used in the artistic decorations. In the hall, rustic green and white baskets were hung from the electroliers [electric chandeliers], filled with exquisitely-arranged sweet peas and foliage, and one huge basket of roses was the theme of many admiring comments.

The article continues in this heady vein for some time, waxing lyrical about floral arrangements, sweet peas, supper in the dining room and a singer called Mr Hoare, who 'furnished' music for dancing. Mr Hoare was actually a banker whom Una, christened Elva, was marrying. Eila's fiancé was the new member of Parliament for the Bay of Plenty, Vernon Reed. You can just imagine young men whispering sweet nothings to beautifully dressed young ladies blushing behind the potted palms, then trying to lure them out through the 'open doors' onto the veranda away from the stern gaze of the deeply conservative TC; there would be no hanky-panky allowed by the chaperones of those young debutantes. On and on it went:

> The hostess wore a rich amethyst chiffon velvet, the bodice almost hidden by lovely lace, fastened with a diamond buckle at the waist, and falling below. Miss Williams's effective frock was of poppy-red chiffon satin, with tight ruched sleeves of the same coloured silk net. Miss Eila wore turquoise silk with wreaths of tiny blue roses and delicate lace, and Miss Una was in white ninon [sheer fabric], the bodice draped with scarves of painted chiffon that fell as a sash to the hem of the skirt, and were bordered with fringes of dull pink velvet.

Not that this was anything like what I had in mind for twenty-first century Te Parae — not unless certain clients were wanting to book a fancy-dress weekend. Anyway, I doubt Te Parae had seen a huge amount of this grandly formal type stuff. Certainly Granny Andy wouldn't have been comfortably swathed in fine taffetas and wreathed in delicate lace; she was usually seen in men's trousers and riding boots, with a silk scarf covering her hair and a roll-your-own ciggie hanging off her lip.

My mother, though, had been entertaining people at Te Parae for years. Dad says that in their first year of marriage Mum played host to 2000 people who visited Te Parae; and to this day she still has the menu for every function she's ever held at the homestead. She was certainly a charming host who could put anyone at ease, be they Princess Anne or the nervous new nanny arriving to look after us boisterous children.

Mum has always been great at organising gatherings, whether for family or for business associates. The birthday parties she put on for Mark and me were no exception. Each July, Mum would organise a fabulous winter-wonderland party for us. She would bake us each a cake, and would invite all the children from the district; somehow she managed to entertain up to 50 children in the middle of winter. The entire district came to our big fifth birthday party. I'm not sure who had the most fun — the kids or the adults. Well, until one of the fathers arrived sporting a great big beard: I took one look at that and the screaming started. My poor mother had to politely ask the gentleman to leave the room, and then calm me down before Mark kicked off too, while the magician entertained the kids.

I look back now and wonder how Mum coped with managing these incredible parties, providing food for all and sundry while trying to keep everyone happy. I'm not sure I would have the patience to do the same . . . But perhaps it was by watching her from an early age that I had learned how to organise events, welcome people and put them at ease.

I find it interesting that I was brought up in this big homestead with three brothers and Mum and Dad, who always had guests, staff staying in the house and people coming to see the horses, plus nannies, but I still had this huge shyness. I couldn't talk to people as a child. I don't know whether it was because I was the only girl, or because my brothers did everything for me. I remember people coming to the house and seeing all these people, but I didn't feel able to talk to them. I wasn't a wuss, but I felt intimidated. If my brothers were there I would step behind them, happy not to be involved. Quiet as a mouse, I was: that's how I got the nickname Mouse, and it stuck.

Sometimes I wonder if it was because Mark, my twin, was very protective towards me. I don't wish to portray him as an angel — he wasn't — but he looked after me much of the time. Once, at primary school, I remember picking my nose when all of a sudden it started bleeding; I promptly fainted at the sight of blood. When I came to, I saw all these faces peering over me and heard someone asking, 'Is she dead?'

I was petrified until I saw Marky kneeling beside me, telling everyone, 'No, she's not dead. She does this all the time.' He just took over, and looked after me. 'Wake up, Bub,' he said. 'You have to get up!' And he stayed with me in the sick bay until Mum arrived to collect me.

I'm certainly not a shy person any more — luckily, because I wouldn't be able to work in hospitality and promotion if I was. But I am reserved in terms of holding back my emotions. It's very hard for me to put my feelings in the public domain. I'm a very private person when it comes to saying what I think about something.

I can't stand frou-frou behaviour, gushing and being overly

dramatic. I get frustrated with how people need to be such drama queens — or kings, for that matter — these days over the most trivial issues. I don't have the time. I can't understand why you'd want to waste your emotions on the small stuff: just get on and do something that's beneficial for others, or for yourself. Maybe some people think I am a bit hard-nosed, maybe I do need to soften up a bit, but it's just not me. It's not me.

***

Probably Mum's biggest challenge in terms of hosting was when royalty came to Te Parae. I don't remember the occasion, but I doubt Princess Anne has forgotten that day. By all accounts she has a good sense of humour, and to listen to my father talk about everything that went wrong I bet, if she does ever think about her visit to the horse stud in the Wairarapa, a wry smile twitches at the corners of her mouth. Anne was still married to Captain Mark Phillips at the time (and Charles was yet to meet Diana). Te Parae was chosen as a destination for Anne and Mark by the Department of Internal Affairs because it was one of New Zealand's leading thoroughbred studs (and close to Wellington) and the royal couple both had a huge interest in horses. While they were at Te Parae, Prince Charles was taken to Brancepeth to be hosted by the Beethams at their historic sheep-and-cattle station.

Geoffrey Palmer was Minister of Internal Affairs, and Dad thought it was 'bloody ridiculous' that protocol demanded he and Mum be introduced to Anne and Mark by a Labour minister whom he'd never met, in his own paddock, on his own property; but he had to mind his Ps and Qs and go with protocol. Today he'll tell you his standout memory is a photo of him and Buzz with the royal couple, and that he's 'horrified at the length of [his] sideboards' — a hairstyle that was fashionable at the time, along with walk shorts and long socks.

Guy was four, Tim was three, and Mark and I were one. We were very often babysat by Diane Rimene, who was married to our stud groom, Mark Rimene. Diane and Mark lived on the other side of the lake, in their cottage, and when we stayed with them she would put us all to bed in a large chest of drawers. It must have looked cute — four little children tucked up snugly in four open drawers, safe as houses. We loved staying over there with them. Mark and Diane were a big part of our early years at Te Parae, so much so that when the local country cop, Pat Shanahan, came out to Te Parae to scope the security for the royal visit, he knocked on the front door and Tim, who was known as Timmy, opened the door. 'What's your name, son?' asked Pat.

'Timmy Rimene,' said the blond-haired, blue-eyed toddler.

'Timmy you may be, but Rimene you sure ain't,' said Pat, who knew Mark Rimene and his family well from their shared interest in rugby, and that Tim Williams was not one of Mark's whanau.

The plan was that Anne and Mark would land in an Air Force Iroquois, with another as backup, to the west of the homestead. So Dad, Buzz and Mark moved all the mares and foals from that area to other paddocks to the east of the stables, some distance from the homestead, so they wouldn't be spooked. This meant the visitors would have a short walk through the garden to the lawn, where the horses could be paraded for them to pat and inspect. But, best-laid plans and all that . . .

Right on time, the helicopters flew over the top of the homestead, ignored the designated landing area close to the lawn, and set down amongst the mares and foals, turning the whole schedule on its head. Dad couldn't believe what was happening.

'I remember thinking the horses would be severely injured, bolting away from the Hueys [Bell UH-1 Iroquois] and crashing through fences. But when we arrived on the scene the horses were staring in amazement at what had just arrived in their paddock and had not moved a muscle.

'Princess Anne and her entourage stepped out of the helicopters and trudged up the hill to be greeted by Minister Palmer and the Williams family and some police who were very concerned at the change of plan.'

Mum's plans had also gone slightly awry. When they had received the letter from Internal Affairs two months in advance, asking if the royal visit was possible, Mum had decided that she'd better refurbish the two main living rooms, and she engaged a Wellington interior decorator for some advice. I'm sure Dad would have looked at the rooms and wondered what she was on about; they would have looked perfectly fine to him, wrinkled scrim lining and all. Nothing major had been done to them since they were first decorated in 1905, but what did he know? Several thousand dollars later, they had two very smart rooms for entertaining. But on the big day the weather had other plans and turned on a brilliant clear day so hot no one wished to sit inside. Anyone who is familiar with Wairarapa weather knows it can never be trusted. Even though the visit was in February, normally a time of settled summer warmth, we can still be caught out by downpours and have outdoor events ruined if we don't have a plan B.

They spent some time discussing the breeding and form of the famous thoroughbreds (information that Anne no doubt took back to her grandmother, the Queen Mother, an avid racing fan) and then, since it was such a lovely warm sunny day, lunch — Mum's menu of caviar and oyster canapés, fillet steak and toffee rum cake — was served outside on the veranda. The princess and her husband never did get to see the newly decorated interior of Te Parae.

If any royalty ever happen to come back, they will find those rooms exactly the same today — they haven't changed a bit. But I'm sure Mum was right: the house would have needed a bit of a facelift after all the visitors they had received over the years.

One of our first nannies, Joanna Meredith, whom we all called JoJo, remembers an 'endless procession of dishes, cleaning up after guests, staff and family as they arrived in droves'. Even though she was only 17 when she started at Te Parae, just out of school and waiting to enrol in nursing training, she learned to make some 'incredible dishes, such as helping Gay create a waterfall of crayfish tails and paua fritters served at the Trentham yearling sales, a classic cheese ball, and the famous duck à l'orange. And I was constantly getting guests a drink.' At five o'clock, no matter what, JoJo had to make everyone a gin and tonic. I guess after a day of chasing, cleaning, entertaining and reprimanding us four children a gin would be the perfect end to the day.

***

I knew this colourful history and experience of entertaining was too good to let it go to waste. It was sad that so many old New Zealand homesteads in this day and age were too expensive to maintain; they couldn't justify their own upkeep, in terms of reroofing, repainting and other continued refurbishments, so they ended up being sold off out of families or, worse, demolished. I also knew that I myself had plenty of experience in various jobs that I might be able to use, to help Te Parae pay for itself. The homestead would be the focus of the business. As Simon and I talked it through, I gradually grew more confident we could make it work as a wedding venue and events centre.

After all, I only had to cast my mind back to a special day I had experienced, when Simon and I exchanged vows right here on the lawns in front of the lake, in 2008. How could I forget the comments from my friends, especially those from the city who had marvelled at the uniqueness of being able to get away from the hustle and noise to relax in rural peace, among family, friends and animals, in my home patch. That made me realise that yes, indeed we could offer something different to bridal couples, and to others who wanted to hold an event such as a corporate retreat, in the peaceful countryside.

It was decided. Goodbye, city; hello, country.

Angela and Simon at their wedding in the grounds of Te Parae. Back row: Simon, Ben Glover, Andrew Kininmonth, Andrew Hopping. Front row: Angela, Caroline Lepionka, Jackie Shaw, Gretch Moylan.

CHAPTER SEVEN

Wedding days

I met Simon when I was 29 and he was 31. My immediate reaction was not the clichéd 'love at first sight' nonsense, but rather (and this is probably a throwback to the country girl in me), I thought to myself, 'He's someone handsome and strong.'

We met through mutual friends Gretchen and Russell Moylan, who were based in Dubai but back visiting New Zealand. Gretchen was at school with me, and Russell went to the same school as Simon. They knew that, like me, Simon loved his racing. I was working for the Auckland Racing Club at the time, and Simon was a police officer.

There was a slight difference in our racing interests: Simon was into harness racing — trotting and pacing — whereas my interests have always been with the gallops (though that's slowly changing). Simon got keen on racing through his father, who did a lot of work with harness horses on a property in Hinds, just out of Ashburton. As a kid Simon used to go to the Reefton races; he would give his grandmother a dollar to place a bet for him, then he'd kick around the grounds, picking up all the discarded totalisator tickets. Back home that night he'd sit by the fire sorting through them, hoping someone had mistakenly thrown away a good one. 'Occasionally I struck it lucky,' he says. He remembers being immersed in the racing scene when he was growing up, 'with the old man watching what was the equivalent of Trackside in those days. Then at secondary school a group of us — three guys they called The Losers because all we did was study the form — would go to Addington Raceway or down to the Merivale TAB and place some bets.'

It wasn't until a year later, when Gretchen and Russell were back visiting again, that we all met up once more. After dinner Simon enquired about upcoming race meetings and our conversation picked up from where it had left off 12 months earlier. That turned out to be the beginning of our future together. Well, that and the fact that he gave me a beautiful leather Oroton wallet for my thirtieth birthday — that's when I thought he must be really serious about me. He probably knew more about luxury brands than I did at that stage. I often joked with him that he was only keen on me because my job with the Racing Club entitled me to an all-access pass on race days. He denied, it of course, but when I later resigned from my position there I'm sure he was a little disappointed. Ironically, back then we never thought we would both end up working in the thoroughbred-breeding industry together.

***

Simon had a unique way of proposing marriage. He may tell the story a little differently, but this is how I recall it. Following a day at the Parnell Tennis Club, drinking Pimm's in the sun, we went back to our little apartment in Grey Lynn. Simon, a little the worse for wear, seemed really keen to present me with a gift he had purchased.

After much fluffing about he produced a beautiful round-cut diamond. He then proceeded to get down on one knee, but just as he was about to pop the question (that much was obvious) he lost his balance, fell over and dropped the diamond, which rolled out of sight. He finally managed to get control of his flailing limbs, but what little romance remained of the evening was lost and he proceeded to crawl into bed, not to surface until the next morning. I then spent the better part of an hour trying to find the diamond. The next morning I gave the jewel back to Simon and suggested he rework his strategy and try again, without the Dutch courage this time. Some months later he achieved a successful result.

We were married in front of a large crowd of family and friends on the lawn at Te Parae. A massive contingent of friends and family chipped in to help, and it was all hands on deck to get the old place shipshape in the week leading up to the big day. Buzz and Susie organised staff from Little Avondale to spend a couple of days weeding gardens, mowing lawns and raking pathways at Te Parae (God only knows who was looking after the 150 horses back at the stud). Anna and James Guild from High Peak Station, great friends of Mum and Dad, arrived four days in advance to help out, too, from feeding the ever-increasing numbers of helpers, to organising the boys to set up the ceremony area, to rounding up the drunken stragglers for the last bus after the wedding.

I could never forget the ladies from the floral world of the Wairarapa. Susie Williams, Didi Abraham, Carol Buchanan, Ricki Savory, Mer Herrick and Di Freeman arrived the day before the wedding with just about every flower known to man and probably pillaged from every garden in the Wairarapa. Here they were creating these floral masterpieces just for our wedding! Mary Bell arrived with chilly bins full of food to feed all of those helping to create this incredible day for us and Eve and Travis Clive Griffin, owners of the top eatery in the Wairarapa, Salute, produced an exquisite four-course menu, working out of a tiny little tent.

Friends of Mum and Dad's, Mick and Annie Deans spent the week building concrete steps up to the house, a task Mum had wanted done for the past five years. Throwing a party is a great excuse to get a place tidied up and odd jobs completed. The two old waka carved by great-grandfather Guy Williams in 1906, which had been in the water ever since, were hoisted out of the lake by family friends Cec and Andy Buchanan. One waka was used as the altar, the other as the bar. This proved such a popular and creative point of difference that we've left them there, and they are used for weddings today. It's something couples love seeing, especially when they hear the story of how great-grandfather Guy milled the trees from the property, then carved the waka to sail on the lake himself.

We turned all seven bedrooms in the homestead over to guests, plus the cottage on the other side of the lake, and they all loved it. Our city friends were so surprised; the ones who hadn't been to Te Parae before knew our family had a historic homestead but I think they were expecting something a little more cottage-y, or maybe at most a villa. Definitely not this huge, rambling homestead surrounded by century-old trees, sweeping lawns, a huge man-made lake and numerous outbuildings to explore. They found their time at Te Parae idyllic — the homely, relaxed atmosphere of the rural setting, and the feeling of being away from it all.

Later, when Simon and I considered our friends' reactions to our own wedding, we thought, If we're going to spend the rest of our days here, why not promote the homestead as a family home away from home destination, and build up a brand? Our minds were made up: we'd move out of Auckland and down to the rural life of Te Parae. There'd be no going back to live in Grey Lynn. But did we really appreciate what sort of lifestyle we were trading in by leaving the city?

Angela's Louis Vuitton handbags.

CHAPTER EIGHT

Selling handbags

'Selling handbags' is a huge understatement when I think about the seven years I spent working for the luxury designer Louis Vuitton on Queen Street in Auckland.

When I joined the company, it had been open for 18 years, so it was well established. At times it felt like I had one of the best jobs in the world (aside from working with horses, of course). At other times, I felt like chucking it all in — such as when some precious individual had thrown all her toys out of the cot; or when I couldn't herd the guests to the private dining room and the chef was on the verge of having a tantrum; or when I spent a whole day trying to get Customs to allow the latest ready-to-wear collection through the borders for an exclusive preview that afternoon, and had to argue with them that the alligator clutch did not require a CITES (Convention on International Trade in Endangered Species) permit — it was only a handbag! But those times were rare.

Every job has its moments, and nothing I had to put up with compared with Simon's work in the police force. When I listened to him talk about the kind of day he'd had, it put my problems into perspective. In the wee small hours we'd be winding down, swapping notes about our work, and he'd talk about policing in South Auckland. It was confronting to hear about the overcrowding, the domestic violence and the child abuse. I'd think, 'That's the balance to my life. He lives it for real, and I live in a very different world.'

The first time I visited Simon's parents, John and Jill Irving, we sat down to dinner in their home in Christchurch. The year was about 2004. Around the table were all the members of their high-achieving family: their eldest son Richard, who was head of English at Auckland Grammar, and his fiancée, Melissa, who became deputy principal of Macleans College — two highly regarded teachers; Simon's sister Anne-Marie, a lawyer, and her husband, Andrew McRae, also a lawyer (and now the Crown Solicitor in Timaru) were there, too. Plus Simon the policeman — and then there was me, a country lass who sold handbags. I looked at Simon's dad and could see him thinking, 'What the heck can I talk to this girl about?'

I couldn't just sit there and let him flounder, trying to dredge up something to say to me. I came to his rescue. I knew he enjoyed his racing even though he prefered the trotters and pacers, so I said, 'I'm into working with horses too. I breed the odd racehorse, and have one racing at the moment.' It worked a treat.

The Irving family have all been very supportive of our move to Te Parae — so much so that every summer Jill and John will come and stay for three weeks and spend all their time helping in the garden!

***

Louis Vuitton may well appear nothing more than Fantasyland for fashionistas to those in the racing industry, but the story of how it became one of the world's most recognisable brands is an inspiring one. The Louis Vuitton brand is copyrighted and incredibly strongly protected, yet it's so popular that it's also one of the world's most counterfeited brands. You can see that LV monogram on many of the company's luxurious products these days — not just handbags. It appears on *Vogue* magazine covers, toted by celebrities, on shoes, watches, jewellery, and accessories such as belts, sunglasses and even books. The price tags seldom dip below four figures, and Louis Vuitton doesn't do discounts.

It's easy to see the glitz and ignore the struggle behind the success. Today Louis Vuitton is a multibillion-dollar corporate — its brand valuation was US$28.4 billion in 2013, to be precise — and it operates in 50 countries with more than 460 stores. When I read about how the original founder, Louis Vuitton himself, started his business, I used to wake up every day feeling proud to stand behind the product.

When I told New Zealanders where I worked, the most common response was, 'That's the company involved with sailing, isn't it?' Not really, but it was an understandable assumption. In 1983 Louis Vuitton first offered a trophy, the Louis Vuitton Cup, to the winner of the challenger series for the America's Cup. Then in 2007 Louis Vuitton changed tack, so to speak, and sponsored the Louis Vuitton Pacific Series and Louis Vuitton Trophy. But Louis Vuitton is about much more than sailing. For their international seasonal promotions, for example, they will think nothing of commissioning a top photographer such as Annie Leibovitz to shoot a model wearing the latest spring collection.

While the Louis Vuitton brand and LV monogram are now among the most powerful brands in the world, Vuitton himself worked his way to the top from nothing. He was born into a poor peasant family in rural France in 1821. His father, Xavier, was a miller who had a very small land-holding, where he had a few animals and grew enough vegetables to feed his family and sell the surplus at the local market. His mother, Corinne, was a milliner who hand-made hats to be sold in the city; she died when Louis was only 10. In 1835, at the age of 13, Louis left home and set off on foot to Paris.

This wasn't unusual. In Europe at that time, it was quite common for young people who were living in poverty to seek their fortune by migrating to the cities, working along the way in return for lodgings. Some survived; others didn't. Louis took two years and reached Paris in 1837. With its population of one million, Paris was already one of Europe's favourite destinations for tourists and, with the railroad completed that year, it was soon to get even busier. Fortuitously, Louis landed an apprenticeship making boxes and trunks (or 'rigid luggage'). He also became very skilled at packing trunks. He would go to the houses of the wealthy who were preparing to travel and carefully fold their garments, and pack their shoes, jewellery, toiletries and brush sets — invaluable experience that came in handy in 1854 when he founded his own company and began making his own special travelling cases.

I compare paintings and etchings of Parisian street scenes from the 1830s, when Louis Vuitton arrived in Paris, with New Zealand at the same time. He was living among architecturally sophisticated buildings and cathedrals, paved streets and a bustling city. Meanwhile, on the other side of the world the city of Auckland was only just being founded; and further south, on the east coast of the North Island, my family would soon be putting down their roots. Compared with the cobbled streets where Vuitton was catering to the Parisian aristocracy, the Williamses and Beethams were struggling along in a semi-wilderness. With mostly horse-drawn buggies for transport in New Zealand in the early 1900s, they would have had to travel with curve-topped trunks, used so that the rain would run off and not settle and soak the contents. I can't help thinking they would have welcomed the chance to own some of Louis Vuitton's flat-topped trunks, which he was the first to design and manufacture in 1858, four years after he started his own business.

The flat-topped trunk was a design that revolutionised the luggage industry. They were easier to stack on journeys and voyages. Vuitton used much lighter-weight materials — at first, grey Trianon canvas, and several years later, a striped canvas. Travellers could pack more clothes into these more practical trunks.

In 1888 Vuitton produced the L. Vuitton symbol for the first time. His business producing sets of matching luggage became highly successful and popular. They produced exquisitely crafted cases for orchestra conductors and for writers such as Ernest Hemingway; a suitcase for the dolls of princesses Elizabeth and Margaret; a beautiful natural cowhide custom-fitted suitcase for Hari Singh, Maharaja of Jammu and Kashmir, with accessories in silver; and suitcases for the safes of the jeweller Cartier.

***

There was no typical day at Louis Vuitton when I worked there; every day brought new surprises. I had started as the administration-cum-office person and then advanced my role into public relations and marketing. Basically I did everything from answering phones to organising the general manager's diary, sorting out staffing issues, including shortlisting candidates and assisting with interviews, distributing press releases, organising local instore events, staff Christmas parties and communications with the Australian and Hong Kong offices, and communicating with media. The role quickly grew into 'you name it, I'll do it' — and that included hosting our top customers.

I'd always check to see if any international celebrities were in town when we were holding a function, and I'd invite them along.

On one occasion I found out the astronaut Buzz Aldrin was staying nearby. I phoned him, my shyness forgotten in my eagerness to get him to a Louis Vuitton event as part of the Louis Vuitton Pacific Series. And, afterwards, I was thrilled to be able to go out for dinner with him and his wife, Lois — although it was Simon who did most of the talking with him. Buzz is not a very tall man — he looks more like anyone's grandad — but he's very forthright, and we had a great time together.

When the movie *The Devil Wears Prada* was released in 2006, I nodded and inwardly smiled all the way through because I could identify with so much of it. I laughed out loud at the line 'A million girls would kill for this job'; Andy Sachs, the protagonist who goes to work for ice-maiden fashion editor Miranda Priestley, has a position that looks so glamorous, but in reality she runs around chasing her tail much of the time. I used to think if I had a dollar for every time someone said, 'You've got the best job in the world,' well . . . Many people would have hated the job and left in a week, but the rewards in terms of what I learned there were enormous, and I could never have learned those skills anywhere else.

When Louis Vuitton staged an event, everything was organised to the most extreme detail. Many of the props were custom made; I couldn't just call up a hire company and order items to be delivered. For instance, there might be special furniture, props, mannequins or coathangers or hanging rails made specifically for Louis Vuitton. If we were holding a party, we'd plan cocktails in special colours for the occasion and they'd have to be tested. The guest lists would be decided, proofread to make sure there were no spelling mistakes, then the invitations would be handwritten by a calligrapher. We'd work out who to invite from local media, a list of who's who, and I'd ensure the RSVPs were followed up so nothing was left to chance. The music was always important —

sometimes a DJ was flown in from Australia or Hong Kong, and organising the catering was a major exercise in menu planning, including tastings.

I found it virtually impossible to sit back and socialise at these big events. I'd be constantly looking around, making sure everything was going smoothly: is the DJ playing the right music to get people dancing? Is the champagne served at a French pour, not a full pour? Are the canapés being passed right around the room, and not being caught only by those at the entrance so the guests elsewhere are missing out? This attention to detail kept me going all night — but that was why Louis Vuitton had the best parties ever.

One of the biggest events I worked at was the Louis Vuitton Pacific Series (LVPS), which was hosted in Auckland as a lead-up to the America's Cup World Series. We were to host many international media, VIPs and Louis Vuitton dignitaries. I had spent weeks visiting different restaurants, wineries and tourist spots throughout Auckland and Waiheke to check suitability for a tour for media attending the event. Christine Belanger was Corporate Events Director for Louis Vuitton, with the LVPS being one of her main events at the time. She was an incredible organiser, peacekeeper and delegator, and someone I learnt a lot from and admired greatly. She worked alongside Bruno Trouble, who was a major part of the management team for the America's Cup and Louis Vuitton Trophy series.

During the series Bruno's wife Melanie was visiting and I was asked to host her for one of the days that there was no sailing. It happened to be Auckland Anniversary, the day the yearling sales started out at Karaka, and my yearling was going through the auction ring that night. I was so nervous as I had no idea what I was going to do with Mrs Trouble, a lady who no doubt would have visited the best restaurants, attended the best parties and probably socialised with the elite of the sailing world! All I wanted to do on my day off was attend the horse sale. Once in the car I cautiously mentioned that I would like to head out to Karaka as I had a yearling being sold that night, hoping that she would not mind being dragged around looking at horses all afternoon. She immediately started telling me about the horses and dogs she had back home and how much she was missing them. Awkwardness abated, we drove out to Karaka, chatting horses all the way. I took Melanie around a few of the hospitality tents, introducing her to many of the thoroughbred fraternity, watched some horses being sold, and before we knew it, it was time to head back into the city so I dropped her back to her hotel. Not only had the day been a success, but I managed to sell my horse for $170,000 that night! For the remainder of the week we spent quite a bit of time together, talking horses, Louis Vuitton and sailing. We continued to keep in touch during my time at Louis Vuitton, even swapping the odd horse photo. A fabulous lady.

Another time we were out hosting some of our clients, and I was seated beside a lovely Japanese couple, who I thought looked rather bored. I was trying desperately to make conversation, talking about the latest collection and asking what they thought of it, and were there any special pieces they admired. I was getting nowhere in a real hurry! I then spotted the man's camera and eventually we got onto their latest travels, and he showed me some photos, including one of a wreck of a World War II fighter plane that he had been diving near. I piped up with some authority and noted it was a Zero, the famous Japanese fighter plane used in that war. Well, his jaw dropped, his face said it all. Why would a Kiwi girl working for Louis Vuitton know what a Zero looks like? I explained my family involvement with vintage aircraft and the Wings Over Wairarapa airshow. From then on it was non-stop talk about planes, to the point where I had exhausted my knowledge and disappeared outside to call Dad to ask him for info on more planes! Needless to say, the couple enjoyed their night and their time with Louis Vuitton.

Of course, things didn't always go to plan: sometimes the goalposts were moved; or someone would throw me a curveball. But I think my Kiwi number-eight wire mentality pulled me through. I never had any disasters. There were a few moments when I felt like bursting into tears, but instead I literally bit the inside of my cheek so hard I drew blood, listened politely when someone was being rude or obnoxious, and took what they were dishing out.

***

I didn't regret signing off from Louis Vuitton, though. I'd been there seven years and I felt it needed fresh ideas. When you work in marketing, unless you're progressing higher in the role I don't think you should stay, because you get stale and run out of ideas. It was time for me to move on. You need to experience new things, understand what your competitors are doing — and I didn't feel I was doing that. And, if truth be told, I'd had enough of being everyone's slave and general dogsbody.

In my last two years there I'd been spending a week every couple of months in Sydney working with the public-relations team, organising media to attend launches of new collections and organise editorial angles for publications. It was intense, to say the least. I'd catch the six pm flight back to Auckland on a Friday, get home, collapse and spend the weekend recovering so I could go back to work on Monday. I worked with two different areas across the Tasman — communication and media, plus client hosting. To put it into perspective, the girl who took over from me lasted less than 18 months. It was extremely hard to keep your wits about you, to concentrate and focus, and it was exhausting. It took the enjoyment out of what, to me, had been a dream job. I certainly appreciate how hard it must be for people who spend their entire time travelling internationally for their business.

***

I've spent quite a lot of time as the only woman in a man's world — growing up with brothers on the farm, and working for the all-male board of Wings Over Wairarapa and for the Auckland Racing Club. I watch with interest media commentary lamenting the lack of female directors on the boards of New Zealand's public companies; only about one in twelve company directors in New Zealand is a woman. A paper published by the Institute of Directors and Business New Zealand showed that companies can be more successful when they have more women on their boards, because women bring a different perspective to men. However, I know from experience and from what other women say to me that we would often rather walk away from confrontation. This is seen as a sign of weakness. I don't see it as a weakness, though; I see it as a strength. Why is humility weak? Why make a scene, mirroring the behaviour of the person or people who are causing problems and delays? At Louis Vuitton, I found it was better to move on, and simply make a mental note not to work with that person in future. 'Deal with it,' I'd tell myself.

It's a good motto for work — and for life.

The cosy smoking room at Te Parae.

CHAPTER NINE

Home to stay

On a bleak, cold, wet day in June 2011 we headed up the winding gravel drive to Te Parae, our new (and my former) home. The trees on either side of the drive were stripped of their leaves; it wasn't exactly a welcoming guard of honour. Not that we were expecting any fanfare. That's not the way of the Williams family.

The move from Auckland had gone smoothly. Fortunately, because Simon was still a police officer on transfer from one region to another, all our moving expenses were paid for by the New Zealand Police. There was none of the stress or hassle of selling property in Auckland: we'd always deliberately rented, although we did grin to each other at one stage, unable to resist reflecting on the irony that we'd probably have been a lot better off financially if we had actually invested in a house, but we weren't really fussed.

Our apartment in Grey Lynn had been the scene of a great social life. It was a small, two-bedroom apartment in a gated community called (funnily enough) The Stables, off Richmond Road in Dickens Street. Originally a beautiful old brick building, it had been converted into residential. After a few months we finally met and made friends with some of the neighbours. That's what makes me laugh about the difference between city living and country life: you can live cheek-by-jowl with other people and not greet each other for six months! But once we had got to know them we found out that of the six flats in the complex, four were occupied by people our age and with the same social circle of friends. So we would all have fun and go out together every weekend. We'd come home from work, walk down the driveway, and if any of the girls were up on their balconies having a wine and a cigarette you couldn't get past them; you had to go up and have a drink. This happened every night.

We called it Melrose Place, after the hit 1990s TV series. There was the token patriarch of The Stables, Brendon, who had lived there for years. I'm sure there were times when he rolled his eyes at us, but he never had a problem with our late nights sitting on the deck, and would often join in for a wine or three. The group of us included Di and Paul Brown, Steph Perrit, Rach Lumsden, Ron Curteis, Jacs Shaw, Speedo (that was Simon's nickname, from when he was a podgy kid at school and not very athletic) and me. Often we would travel in a group for weekends away, up to Pakiri to ride horses, over to Waiheke to sample the latest vintage from the local wineries, or even venturing to the good old Lime Bar for a few quiet drinks and a sing-along to old-school songs after a day on the punt at Ellerslie or Avondale. One year we celebrated Christmas by taking a tour of the vineyards out west of Auckland — well, that was the intention. In reality we only managed two wineries! By the time we reached the second one and were sitting by the lakeside sipping rosé, there was no way any of us was leaving until closing time.

Besides, the lake was too inviting: next minute some of our party were taking a quick dip — much to the disapproval of management.

Life was good, life was simple. This was long before responsibilities set in — marriage, babies and serious careers. We had nothing domestic to hold us back. Our garden was a little lemon tree in one planter box on the deck by our outdoor furniture set. That was it. No lawns. No watering. No animals. We did what we liked. And yet come Friday night we thought we were exhausted and we'd be thinking, 'Oh, on Saturday we'll watch a bit of *Trackside*, or maybe go to the races if we're up to it.' That might be our big decision for the day. There might be a new restaurant opening in Ponsonby: should we go to that or somewhere else for dinner? Maybe to a café in Jervois Road? Or was there a concert on somewhere? We didn't go to plays — that wasn't our thing — but festivals, yes, or down to the waterfront for a wander around and off to Newmarket shopping. The only place I stayed away from in the weekends was Queen Street and that was because I worked there during the week.

Our life was so free and easy. Little did I know how much it was going to change.

***

How can I ever forget that day? Even though we'd moved down to the Wairarapa in the middle of a freezing-cold winter, it felt good to be coming home to stay.

We pulled up in front of the imposing wooden entrance. Sparkle Bear, my faithful old Labrador, who'd been waiting 10 years for me to come home, was wagging her tail, happy to greet us in our new home. I hugged her and she waddled inside after us, through the front door and the downstairs hallway to where Mum and Dad were waiting. I'd been through this entrance millions of times since Mum

Angela's great grandmother, Eileen Williams (née Hope-Lewis), who was a champion golfer, in Christchurch in 1904.

Top to bottom: A yearling parade on the Te Parae lawn, 1960s;
WaitAMinute winning the Covers and Others Maiden at Ellerslie, December 2003.

The Williams family. Left to right: Guy, Tom (standing), Tim, Mark, Gay, Angela.

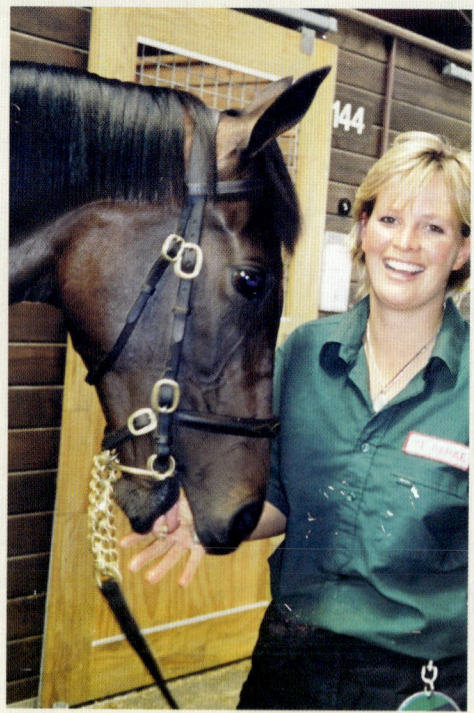

Top to bottom: Angela and Sandy at the Wairarapa A&P show, 1984; Angela with a yearling at the Karaka sales, January 1999.

Top to bottom: Hector Rodriguez taking a nap; Hine Waka and Brian the fawn.

Top to bottom: The large entertaining room at Te Parae, known as 'The Big Room'; the Ferrari luncheon at Te Parae in 2014.

Angela at work in the garden.

Angela with Boo and Hine-Waka, looking back over the lake to Te Parae homestead.

and Dad had brought me home as a newborn baby, and I'd always taken all the splendour for granted: the native-wood tongue-and-groove lining in matai, totara and rimu; the massive double-door chest with all our old sports gear chucked inside where we'd left it — stuff going back to my grandfather's days, including his leather boxing gloves; an old Box Brownie camera in a leather case, and even an early movie camera; and goodness knows what other old treasures. But now it felt as if I was walking back into the house in a different way; I had a new responsibility. I wasn't exactly about to re-create something new — just breathe a second (or was that fourth?) life into the place.

While Mum made a warming lunch, Simon and I unloaded the car and carried some of our stuff upstairs. The hallway up there was enormous — big enough for us kids to play cricket in when Mum used to lock us up there with a little gate across the top of the stairs. Out of habit I turned right at the top of the stairs, towards my little corner bedroom, still exactly the same as when I'd slept there as a child — frilly curtains, brightly coloured walls, double doors opening through to my twin brother's room. All our children's books — and all those from earlier generations — were still stacked in the bookcases.

And, most treasured, a rare family heirloom, occasionally brought out to show an interested visitor: *A Letter To The Right Hon. W. E. Gladstone: Being An Appeal On Behalf Of The Ngatiraukawa Tribe*, by T. C. Williams. This book, dating from 1873, is all hand cut. It is slightly moisture damaged and foxed. It dates back to my great-great-great-grandfather Henry Williams, and it provides some insight into the personal observations he passed on to his son TC about the Treaty of Waitangi and why he, Henry, became involved in its signing. This sense of history — along with Henry's old Bibles — is so important to Te Parae. I knew when I touched base with these treasures again that I'd made the right decision in coming back.

Along the hallway are more cupboards, storage rooms, two bathrooms and seven bedrooms with double-hung windows that open out on to the roofs of the verandas below. I called out to Simon and pointed out of the window in the bathroom. 'When we were children, Mum and Dad were returning from an overseas trip to look at horses. The nanny had bathed us and got us all ready to greet them. She was having her own bath with the window open when Tim climbed up on this roof and threw a live eel in through the window. You can imagine what happened when the eel hit the hot water — the nanny levitated!'

So many memories came flooding back as I walked around the homestead. I had such a happy childhood growing up here. There were a few ups and down of course, but we'd been brought up to be strong, to weather the storms. Three generations of my family had lived in this rambling wooden building.

I thought back to the parties, the events, and all the visitors who had streamed through these doors. Yearling parades were held here on the lawn each January, before cousin Sam moved on to the Little Avondale Stud, closer to Masterton. It was such a grand affair. I was just a little kid but I have the photographs as records: the yearlings all glossy and showing off, led from the stables, supervised by studmaster Mark Rimene, past the gardens and the rosebeds in full bloom, and on to the big lawn on the west side of the house. There would be hundreds of people watching, seated on haybales; they travelled here from Wellington, Manawatu, Hawke's Bay, and some from as far as Auckland.

I looked at the accumulation of furniture, books, paintings and other things, added to over the years, casually on display in the house: the stag's head in the hallway, shot by my grandmother Nancy when she was on her honeymoon in 1938 in North Canterbury; paintings by my great-aunt Maude Burge (née Williams) who studied under Charles Frederick Goldie before going on to paint in Europe with Frances Hodgkins; the paintings in the smoking room of Te Parae's prize-winning stallions dating back to the 1940s, along with photographs of wins by horses bred by or purchased from Te Parae.

I wandered around the outside, through the gardens, and in and out of the rooms downstairs from the lower hallway to the Big Room, where visitors were always struck by the view through the bay windows of great-grandfather Guy's lake. This room, with its wooden fireplace said to be carved by one of Maude's sisters, Elfie, was full of antique pieces of furniture inlaid with walnut and maple brought out from England, a book cabinet with Bibles dating back to the 1800s, and Maori artefacts gifted to my ancestors.

In the dining room, there was that view to the lake again — this time through double doors that, in summer, are thrown back so guests can spill out onto the veranda to smoke after dinner. Around the walls hang paintings: Henry Williams above an antique sideboard; his son Thomas Coldham Williams in his top hat (which is still upstairs in the massive tallboy in Simon's dressing room); Guy Williams, who built Te Parae; his son, my grandfather Alister (all these grandfathers!) above the piano; and a portrait of Mum and Dad. Mum is one of only two women on these walls; the other is Annie Beetham, who married TC Williams. We never ate in this room as kids; we were fed in the kitchen. This was kept for formal dining.

Through another door is the pantry, all white-painted match lining with scrubbed wooden benchtops and high cupboards, where I've found boxes of old cans of turtle soup and ancient preserves — pear mince, mandarin liqueur and gooseberry sauce. Whenever I clean out all these cupboards I wonder if Te Papa museum might have a use for some of the stuff I've discovered: a remedy for whooping cough, for instance, in an elaborately decorated container and a quaintly designed bottle of chloroform. 'What was that used for?' I wondered aloud as I pulled it out of an unlocked cupboard we children must have toddled past thousands of times while pottering around upstairs. Nothing, it seems, had been thrown away: it is a treasure trove of stuff built up over more than a century.

***

Mum and Dad would be staying for a while, then it would be just Simon and me rattling around in this huge, glorious place. We'd left the city and all its comforts behind forever. No more modern, warm rooms. In Auckland if I felt the cold I could flick a switch and central heating would warm me through. No more texting the café in Ponsonby to have my latte waiting for me to collect on the way to work.

It didn't help that we'd arrived in the middle of a winter on steroids — Wairarapa had a massive snow dump in August 2011, the likes of which had not been seen, according to locals, since 1935, and some farmers were snowed in for three days. My determination not to lose my sense of style went straight out the door. It was off with the nice sheer tights, skirts and designer tops, and on with all the winter gear — the woolly socks, massive jerseys, pompom hats and Michelin Man trousers — that I could find in our childhood bedrooms. It wasn't that I was expecting to wear my Auckland designer wear every day — I knew what sensible country clothing consisted of — but really and truly, even though we'd only driven from Auckland to Wairarapa, you'd think we'd moved from Tahiti to Dunedin, such was the change in climate. I gave silent thanks to Mum for not throwing anything away.

Even with all the winter woollies, though, I was damn cold.

When I thought back, I realised I should have seen this coming. I remembered once, on a visit home, seeing Mum — my beautiful, glamorous mother, who could look a million dollars if she wore a jute feedsack snatched out of the stables — sitting up in bed with a Russian-style woollen hat pulled down and tied tightly under her chin. 'Mum!' I'd exclaimed, appalled at her slipping standards. 'How could you wear that thing?' I should have known by now that there was no baseline when style gave way to comfort.

Those first weeks back home, for me, were like a bird being freed from a cage. Strangely, I didn't miss the city at all. For one thing I didn't have to put on makeup every day, and that made me extremely relieved. Mum had taught me from a young age that wearing makeup every day is not ideal; you should let your skin breathe.

And then there was the immense quiet. It may seem strange to city folk, but I struggled to get to sleep at night at first because the silence was so deafening. It was as if there was absolutely no noise. And when there was no moon it was really pitch black: there were no street lights. I hadn't realised how accustomed I'd become to falling asleep to traffic noise, people getting in and out of taxis, shouting, giggling, bottles being put out in the rubbish — all that night rowdiness that country people find intolerable.

My thoughts turned to how we were going to stay warm; and, more importantly, how quickly Simon and I could get cracking on this place and open it up for business. I could envisage everything I wanted to do. I could see right in front of me that here was a big chunk of history that I'd always taken for granted, but that clients and visitors would love to see and know more about.

And then there was much more to Te Parae than the Williams dynasty — more than Henry Williams, horses, hunting deer and breaking in pasture. There was also quite a famous artistic side to our family, which could be traced back to the Beethams. Legend has it that William Beetham was once portrait painter to Russian royalty in St Petersburg, and he had exhibited at the Royal Academy in London.

William's talents were passed down to Annie and TC's daughter, my great-aunt Maude, who made a name for herself internationally as Maude Burge. Two beautiful paintings of hers hang in the Big Room at Te Parae. Maude might have been a nineteenth-century woman, but she certainly was not afraid to march out on her own and take herself off in a new direction. She studied at the Wellington School of Design, which was set up in 1886 by the Wellington Board of Education under the direction of Arthur Dewhurst Riley, a passionate man who went around the lower North Island giving talks about the importance of 'manual' education and how crucial it was for students to learn how to draw properly and not just copy others. In a speech he gave in Masterton in 1890, he pointed out that, 'Ladies who became proficient in drawing [could] earn their own living in any part of the world.' And that is what Maude went and did, as mentioned earlier.

There is another painting by Maude, in the Fletcher Trust Collection, of her sister Githa. Githa had married Admiral Sir James Fergusson, brother of Sir Charles Fergusson, who was governor-general of New Zealand from 1924 to 1930. The Fergussons were intimately connected with Te Parae and often visited over the decades. Charles's son Bernard, years later, become the last British-born governor-general of New Zealand in 1962. As a young boy he came to stay at Te Parae, and turned up for breakfast one morning in bare feet. Apparently my stern great-grandfather Guy growled at him, 'What would your father say, young man, if I turned up at breakfast without my shoes on?' Bernard simply replied, 'He would be far too polite, sir, to remark on the fact.' Just recently, we hosted Margaret and George Fergusson, who is Bernard's son and the

Governor of Bermuda. So the connection continues. George was so happy to look back at our visitor book and see both his father and his grandfather note their visits to Te Parae.

When I think about the women in my family who've gone before me, and the times in which they were raised — strict Victorian times — I'm encouraged that Maude, brought up when you didn't go barefoot even at breakfast, had the fortitude to make it on her own internationally as a painter. Perhaps, like me, when she sailed away from Auckland at a young age, leaving behind that wonderfully privileged social life, she lay awake at night wondering if she'd done the right thing.

Anyway, sadly, the talent stopped with Maude: my painting skills are limited to slapping all-weather acrylic on the outside of the stables or to touching up the windowsills.

***

It was quite a surreal moment for me when I realised all this history that I'd grown up with was also New Zealand's history — a legacy. It was a great contribution to an understanding of more than a century of farming life; and we could use it as a backdrop to our venture. I felt a freedom from the stress of indecision, and a sense of excitement and relief that we had made the move. The decision was correct. It felt right to be back.

Now what I had to do was think about how, exactly, all my experience in hospitality, accumulated since I'd left school at 18, could help to turn this homestead into a successful business.

Rachel, Angela and Lizzy at Down House.

CHAPTER TEN

My big OE

I'd grown up in a household where it was normal to have at least two or three extra people at our table, and often staying overnight. But where had my passion for hosting people for a living really started?

Right from the word go it had always been Mum and Dad — Tom and Gay Williams — who'd influenced every single thing I had done. They were very much a part of my life, no question about that. In my last year at Wanganui Collegiate, Mum pushed me to do a gap year in the UK. I didn't really know what I wanted to do or be when I left school, so it was Mum who wrote letters to schools and found one that she thought would suit: Down House in Berkshire.

Down House accepted me and I went there for one year, until I was 19. Not that this gap year made any difference to my attitude in terms of the direction I wanted to go in life. While I was at Down House I worked alongside two Australian girls, Lizzie and Rachel. Our roles were to help the teaching staff with activities, work in the physical-education department, and help with the general supervision of boarding houses for the younger kids. There were about 15 of us, boys and girls, from our final year at Collegiate who went to the UK for a year, including Mark. We all left Auckland in early January 1992 and headed to Hawaii for a two-day stopover en route. I look back now and think, What the hell were our parents thinking, letting these 18-year-olds loose on the world? Many of us had not gone further from home than Australia, and yet here we were in Hawaii for two days — freedom! Of course there was the motor-scooter accident by one of the boys — not serious enough to go home but maybe a wake-up call to show a little more responsibility We all thought Hawaii was incredible: the beaches, the shopping, the glitz and glamour of Honolulu at night. We left Hawaii in our summer shorts and T-shirts and flew in to Gatwick late in the afternoon on a miserable January day — what a shock! We raced into the airport bathrooms to layer up before heading out into the freezing-cold UK winter, said our goodbyes and headed off to our respective schools. Even though we were dotted all over the UK, most of us managed to fit in a bit of travel to visit each other and experience different schools.

When I'd finished my year at Down House, Mum and Dad suggested I get some qualifications in cooking at a Prue Leith course. I didn't especially love cooking, and had no burning ambition to be a chef. I did cook a lot at home, but only because Mum did. But this is how Mum and Dad operated with us kids; it's how they had lived their lives — they saw opportunities for us and they would push us to take them. Dad said, 'You are on the other side of the world, so take the chance while you have it. Don't come back here then regret that you haven't done all the things you might have done. Go to Leiths. Don't come straight back now.'

I thought, 'Okay, if you think it's a good idea, I'll do it.' I look back now and I'm so grateful to them for suggesting I get the qualifications, rather than faff around waitressing or working in a bar, which I could so easily have done.

I completed a four-month course at the Leiths School of Food and Wine, founded by Prue Leith. It was one of the leading London cookery schools at the time — and it probably still is. Prue Leith was a real inspiration. Born in South Africa in 1940, she started out providing lunches to top-level businesses. She sold her Michelin-starred restaurant, Leith's, and the cookery school in the 1990s, by which time her turnover was more than £15 million a year. She'd also found the time to write novels, and she was a newspaper food columnist.

It's fair to say I wasn't a star pupil at Leiths. I was living (dossing) in a two-bedroom flat with about six other Kiwis. The course was expensive and I didn't have a lot of cash left over for other expenses. The first job I managed to snare when I finished was at a party given by a family at Wimbledon. I was under the impression I was going to be doing canapés, hors d'oeuvres, that sort of thing, but when I arrived I was told to make these new cocktails called Cosmopolitans. I'd never heard of them — I hadn't even consumed a cocktail at the age of 19, let alone been taught to create one. Thank goodness everyone was so drunk they didn't care about the concoction I served up. 'Oh, let's have another one,' they shouted, reeling about. I had no idea of the correct recipe; I was just throwing all this alcohol into a blender. I tasted it and it was ghastly. They thought so too. 'Oh, it tastes terrible,' they said, but it didn't stop them from drinking it. 'Are you sure you went to cooking school?' somebody asked me at some stage in the proceedings. I thought I'd really stuffed up. I needed the money because I had to get out of London and that dreadful flat. I did get paid, but they probably never went back to Leiths again for a caterer.

The main reason I was desperate to get out of London was that the city was too expensive for me. After I graduated from Leiths I'd seen a job advertised in Northumberland for a chef/cook in a bed and breakfast. I'd never been to Northumberland but I thought, 'That's far enough out of London for me.' As soon as I got accepted I jumped on the train and tootled on up. I lasted about four months. The name of this bed and breakfast will stay unpublished. The boss was a taskmaster — tough and strict. I started at the bottom and stayed at the bottom, and I reckon if I was working there today I'd still be at the bottom. I worked from five in the morning until nine at night, doing breakfast from scratch. I did classics such as kedgeree, cooking the rice first, boiling the eggs, adding smoked fish. Try getting up before dawn and cooking mackerel on an empty stomach! I also had to prepare the hors d'oeuvres and the three-course meals for the evening, and serve them, plus serve the wine in between — and do lunch for my bosses. I spent my break walking to Corbridge, the local village, for some fresh air and to get out of the kitchen.

It was my jumping-off point into the industry, one of those jobs where you are treated like (how to put this politely?) the most junior, but if you can stick it out without complaining, and work really long hours, you will learn a lot and gain from it. For instance, I quickly learned the high standards required by owner–operators in the hospo world of English bed and breakfasts. It was my introduction to fussy customers and, as I was rightly told, 'A customer is not someone to argue or match wits with. Nobody ever won an argument with a customer.' I've never forgotten that, and it's stood me in good stead.

That's also where I quickly learned to cart *Leiths Cookery Bible* around with me everywhere I go. I still use it to this day, for everyday meals at Te Parae and for every wedding — even though the pages are coming away from the cover, the binding is shot and it's held together with sellotape. I've written notes all through it. Mum and I argue — she has the *Constance Spry Cookery Book* from the 1950s, which she swears is her bible and reckons is better, but I disagree.

There was another lesson I learned during my gap year, which is also important in the hospo industry. Down House sent me for a couple of months to a school in Ireland, County West Meath, where the classrooms were prefabs and I pretty much had to take over as PE teacher. It was great fun. All the junior boys wanted to know about rugby and I had no idea of the rules, despite having three brothers. At lunchtimes some of the younger teachers would take me down to the pub, where farmers turned up on tractors, and we'd get chatting. I told them once that I got called Mouse, and from then on all these old gummers sitting at the bar in their shabby gear would see me coming and call out, 'Halloo, Moose,' then rattle on in their Irish accents.

I learned how to drink Guinness, but that's not all. More importantly, I learned not to judge people by their appearances. Those farmers might have looked all gruff and growly, but if you sat down and started talking to them they were such charming gentlemen, and so interested in your day, and always really funny and amusing.

***

If I had thought I had it hard in Northumberland, it was nothing compared to what my great-aunt Hilda Williams, sister of Maude and Guy, achieved when she set out on her OE a year before World War I broke out. She was an amazing woman. Like Maude, she was a painter and trained at the Wellington School of Design; she wasn't as successful, though she did exhibit a bit in Christchurch later in life.

The fourth child of TC and Annie, Hilda was a heroine in terms of what she did for soldiers in the Great War. I had no idea my great-aunt had led such a remarkable life until I stumbled across her obituary when preparing material for this book. I knew she'd never married, and I always thought she'd left New Zealand for England, led the sheltered life of a somewhat privileged Victorian lady, then returned to settle in Canterbury society to play bridge. But I was wrong. True to Williams tradition she, too, was another strong-minded, determined individual willing to change direction when she saw a need. When Hilda died on 21 December 1939, her obituary in the *Evening Post* said the news would be received 'with profound regret not only by personal friends and friends of her family, but in all parts of the Dominion by thousands of returned soldiers whom she befriended during the Great War'.

What could this mean?

When war broke out the year after she arrived in London, she cast her eye around for something useful to do. She was one of the first to see that New Zealand soldiers desperately needed somewhere decent to stay when they were on leave or invalided out of Gallipoli, France and Egypt. Being a daughter of TC Williams, she had plenty of connections, and she wasn't afraid to use them. She set to work and, with her sister Ethel and Ethel's husband, Arthur Russell, formed a committee. They commandeered four big houses in the Bloomsbury area — three in Russell Square and one in Upper Bedford Place.

There was a New Zealand connection with the house at 23 Russell Square. It was owned by Sir Alexander Rendel, who had married Eliza Hobson, daughter of Governor Hobson. This is most likely how Hilda gained access to these prime addresses; she would have met Hobson in Wellington and made contact when she was in London, and through Rendel's contacts she had convinced the military authorities of the need for such establishments. It would not have been an easy task: Russell Square has always been prime London real estate. Nevertheless Hilda had these grand houses converted into hostels for the men to use for R&R. When the soldiers arrived from the front, filthy and exhausted, there were large bins for them to dump their clothes in to be laundered, then they could step into a hot shower and a plunge bath. The unlimited hot water must have seemed like heaven after the nightmare of the trenches. Freshly bathed, shaved and into clean clothes, the soldiers could then go upstairs to eat and socialise in the canteen. The *Christchurch Press* reported:

> The colour scheme of the canteen is chiefly violet, and accordingly the ladies wear overalls of violet linen, with cuffs and collars of black silk finished with white, and fastening with waist-belts of shiny black leather . . . Whether stationed in kitchen or canteen, these voluntary helpers will know they are doing valuable work.

Up another flight of stairs on the next level was a reading and writing room, a billiards room, and bedrooms with 60 beds.

Hilda went on to set up more canteens for New Zealanders in London. One called The Dug-Out at 3 Victoria Street got off to a great start when the High Commissioner Lord Plunket and other officials from the New Zealand War Contingent Association were among the first to patronise the joint. Soldiers came along each day to read papers, play games and 'take light refreshment'.

To give the men a Christmas treat in 1916, Hilda 'hit on the happy idea' to invite a special guest to The Dug-Out, Corporal Cyril Bassett VC, the first and only New Zealander to be awarded the Victoria Cross in the Gallipoli campaign. Corporal Bassett came as a guest of honour to cheer up the men, 'and at the same time afford all the excuse for a little Christmas jollification'. She baked a large cake, iced it with 'Corporal Bassett, VC' and tied around it the ribbons of the VC and DCM (as two DCM men were also present).

Hilda was an extraordinary woman with limitless energy. Two years after she closed The Dug-Out, she opened another, larger canteen in Hornchurch, in nearby Beethoven House, as an adjunct to a hospital established for convalescing New Zealand troops. She called it Te Whare Puni. By the end of the war, some 20,000 New Zealand soldiers had passed through that hospital; many of them would have visited Hilda's canteen. While she was there she also became involved in, as the *Dominion Post* put it, 'fitting up limbless soldiers'.

Her good works did not go unrecognised. In the 1918 King's Birthday and New Year Honours List, Hilda Williams was given the award of an Officer of the Order of the British Empire for war services.

Good old Hilda — little did she know that a hundred years later, at Te Parae, a Williams girl would once more be running around welcoming people, hosting them and providing them with food and drink. This time around, however, those on the receiving end would be paying guests, not weary soldiers serving their country.

Angela, Sam Williams and Kim Bone at Checkpoint Charlie, Berlin.

CHAPTER ELEVEN

Scotland

No matter how tough my Northumberland bosses might have been, it wasn't enough to give me all the skills needed to pull together every loose end at a Te Parae country wedding; things could so easily unravel, like dropped stitches in a home-knitted jersey, despite the best-laid plans.

After my stint at the bed and breakfast I wasn't really ready to return to New Zealand, so I hooked up with my cousin Sam and three of his school friends, Dave Chadwick, Kim Bone and Chook Ellingham, who had all bought an old Kombi van, and we did a five-week tour of Europe. I had been through the Continent before, during my gap year, by train with some girlfriends from Collegiate Gretch Haynes, Emma Scott, Bridget Carver and Kirsty Hansen. This time round was completely different, though. It wasn't exactly a cultural tour; I think the boys were expecting me to be chief cook while they concentrated on getting to the next Beerfest or bar before closing time. But we had a great time, despite my being the only girl.

Then, of course, it was time to earn some more money. I spent some time cooking for families in Scotland — hardworking farming folk with young children. An English woman called Caroline Milne-Hume, who had worked as a groom at Te Parae a few years earlier, had stayed in contact with our family after she married, had a family and went to live in Scotland. I stayed with her and her husband Patrick in Kinross, and used their house as my base. I would cook for them and babysit their three young children. Sometimes they would 'farm' me out to work for their friends; for instance, I went and worked for their relations in Aberdeen for a while, and did a lambing beat there. Mark and I both spent a lot of time with the Milne-Hume family; it was our home away from home. We spent Christmas there and helped out where we could. They and their friends liked having me there because I came from a New Zealand farm, and their houses were like typical Kiwi farmhouses — except that they cooked on Agas. They kept the Agas going all day, which I loved because it was so cold.

I'd move from house to house like some sort of kitchen babysitter, working for different families, filling up people's freezers with meals; or I'd assist mums who worked on farms and had young children and didn't have time to put a meal on the table. I was 19, and I saw how hard these women with families worked; they were doing two fulltime jobs.

I was developing a reputation for turning out good comfort food for families, particularly farming ones — the bulky lamb pies, lasagnes, all this stuff from *Leiths Cookery Bible*. And if I couldn't think what to make I would fax Mum and ask her for ideas: 'Mum, I have to cater for a dinner party for 10 people. What shall I cook?' She would fax back all these recipes for me. (This was before the days of email and text messaging and Skype!) She would have been busy all hours of the night working out what I should serve, how I should present all the dishes, and she would have typed it all out for me. She basically organised, from New Zealand, many of the menus I was called on to prepare. I couldn't have managed without her. Her dishes were really practical: they were ones that children liked, such as chicken goujon (strips of chicken battered and fried meatballs stuffed with mozzarella and mini scotch eggs), and they could go in the freezer.

I recall, one time, going to a family's holiday house in the hills of Aberdeen and being asked to prepare high tea for a family member's seventieth birthday party. The trouble was, the kitchen in the holiday house had very limited cooking equipment: there weren't even any measuring spoons or mixing bowls. I don't think the kitchen was used a great deal! I had to think hard, and the number-eight wire mentality came into play. I used the family china for mixing bowls and the cutlery for measuring and mixing; I made cake-baking tins out of truckloads of tinfoil, in all shapes and designs; and I lit a fire in the old range to bake things. Fortunately, all of this worked just fine — it's amazing what you can do under pressure.

After a while I got sick to death of being in the kitchen, so the lambing beat was a welcome change. Lambing over there is a bit different from in New Zealand. It's very intensive, with all the ewes lambed in sheds; and you have to actually be in there with them when they're lambing. It was not quite what I was used to in New Zealand, where our sheep deliver their lambs outside in all weather, but it was a great experience to see how they farm. I loved Scotland, even though it was freezing cold — bitter but beautiful. If I went to live over in the UK now, it would be in Scotland rather than London.

***

Much as I appreciated the support from Mum and Dad in grabbing these opportunities on the other side of the world, I was missing home. Every Kiwi who's been on the other side of the world will understand that feeling: the way your ears perk up when you hear a New Zealand accent, watch a rugby game on television, or meet up with expats in a pub.

By now it was 1994. I packed up my meagre belongings and headed for Heathrow. I didn't have a clue what job awaited me in New Zealand, or how I'd make my living. What I was sure of was that, after my British experience, I wasn't too proud or too scared to turn my hand to any task, no matter how tough, dirty or back-breaking, or how demanding the customer.

I would soon find out, though, that it's not just the lowest-ranked job in a kitchen that's bone-tiring and tough. In a few years' time I'd be in a dream job, immersed in luxury design and high fashion, ordering fine champagne and perfectly catered canapés, but nonetheless working 10 times harder than in my days as a short-order cook dishing up kedgeree.

At Kekerengu Store. Left to right: Julia Dillon, Angela, Richard Macfarlane, Sanc Macfarlane, Suzie Macfarlane.

CHAPTER TWELVE

Down South

I didn't go home to Te Parae straight away. Of course I called in, dumped my stuff, said hello to Ma and Pa, the dogs, horses and everyone, but then I headed down to Queenstown, because that was where the jobs and the money were. Snow equals skiing; and skiing equals people wanting food, drinks and plenty of fun — and they're willing to pay for it.

I went there with no money and left after 18 months with no money, having worked all the time in the Lone Star restaurant and bar under the leadership of James 'Chief' Whelan, co-founder of the Lone Star brand. The height of summer and winter are both peak seasons in Queenstown; it was frantically busy — and totally different from slaving at the bed and breakfast and filling freezers in Scotland. I was given a couple of days off during the week, which meant an afternoon spent on the ski slopes of the Remarkables or driving over to Cardrona, or pretending to be a photographer with my flatmate Sally Jamieson and taking photographs of big tour groups at the bottom of the gondola. Queenstown can be a little insular, so on the odd occasion I would hitch a ride with Jas Miller, who was then a driver with NZ Couriers, taking the scenic route from Queenstown to Christchurch overnight and returning the next day. During the winter the mountain passes were often closed to cars, but we would always manage to get through, even with snow scraping the axles of the big 16-wheeler. It was a beautiful sight, coming over the Lindis Pass as dawn was breaking, with pure white snow all around and not a soul in sight.

Another one of our flatties, Annabel Tapley, worked at Shotover Jet for a while, and dragged us into filling seats on the jetboat when new drivers were being trained. That was a hair-raising experience — fast and furious, the scenery passing in a blur. It was a great opportunity, but I don't remember much about it, and I only did it once.

I do recall not being really satisfied with my time in Queenstown. Somehow I knew it was time for a change of direction; I needed to learn something else. I was restless, without really knowing why. Perhaps I was just sick and tired of being stuck inside a kitchen all day, cooking, cooking, cooking.

So what did I do? Got a job in another kitchen.

I got a request, via Mum, from family friends in Kaikoura, Susie and Richard Macfarlane, who own Winterhome Garden, right on State Highway 1. Would I help them out and work for them over the summer? Richard and Susie were converting The Store, Kekerengu, into a café and needed help. So up I went from Queenstown to Kaikoura. When I got there and started, I silently gave thanks that I had worked so hard all those months in Northumberland because, if I hadn't, this would have been a huge shock. The café conversion was still in the early stages; my day consisted of walking across planks of wood balanced on sawhorses, carrying trays of beautiful home-made, fresh-out-of-the-oven muffins. Trouble was, the café was the main refreshment stop for the buses coming off the Picton ferry, and back in those days all the passengers wanted was pies and chips!

For three long, hot summer months I worked seven days a week, and I lived in The Store itself. This building was just 50 metres from the sea, but not once did I have time to have a swim; my togs didn't even get unpacked from my suitcase. The job was huge and it was really hard graft. I don't think I have ever seen anyone work harder than Susie and Richard, turning a grotty old dairy into one of the must-see cafés along the Kaikoura coast. They took a risk and showed huge determination. Looking back now I can see what an experience it was for me to be a part of that transformation. But right there and then I realised I did not want to be stuck in a kitchen for the rest of my life; I couldn't bear being cooped up in an inside job any longer. I stuck it out for as long as I had committed myself to Richard and Susie, then I said goodbye and came home to Te Parae, to the homestead; back to the horses and the outdoors. This time my career would have a complete change in direction. I would go in the direction where my twin brother Mark was going — off to university.

Mark was already at Massey University in Palmerston North, well into his study of turf management. I decided to join him; and, because I'd been brought up with animals and loved working with them, I enrolled in a veterinary nursing course. I studied and worked at the vet clinic at Massey, experiencing all kinds of weird and wonderful things, from X-raying a sedated tiger from Wellington Zoo, to splinting the damaged wing on a cockatoo, to running away from a wild seal! After two years I graduated with a diploma and went to work in Masterton for the South Wairarapa Veterinary Association.

I still wasn't wildly happy in my new career, even if I was surrounded by animals and back living at home in the Wairarapa for the next two years. I could now be with my horses again, relax with Mum and Dad, my Masterton mates and my extended family. But, even though I knew I didn't want to be in a kitchen cooking, I did feel I needed more stimulation in terms of using the hospitality experience I'd gained abroad. I missed the pleasure I got out of welcoming and entertaining people, and making them feel happy. I was starting to sense that this was my calling in life.

But then something happened which would change all of our lives for ever. Out of the blue, our happy, close-knit family would be struck by tragedy, and in an instant I would be forced to grow up, stop drifting through my life, and make some tough decisions. It began with a telephone call.

Angela's twin brother, Mark Charles Williams.

CHAPTER THIRTEEN

Mark

How do we know what to do when we're forced to cope with loss? Every person behaves differently. I'm not a particularly emotional person — I don't wear my heart on my sleeve — but I'm enormously proud of my family, of the way my parents coped right from the moment the telephone rang on 20 December 1998.

I'll never forget that day. I was 25 years old and living back at Te Parae while working at the vet clinic in Masterton. It was a summer morning and I was up early to feed the horses before I went to work. I'd come back into the kitchen for breakfast. One look at Dad's face told me something terrible had happened; he looked incredibly distressed. Then he said the words that turned my world upside down: 'I've just had a call from James Innes, who owns the helicopter company over in America where Mark's working. The chopper with the boys is missing. He doesn't know where they are but they're trying to locate them.'

'The boys' included my twin brother, Mark, who'd left New Zealand a few months earlier for a working holiday doing what he loved: live capture of wild animals from helicopters. He'd gone to the US after achieving a Bachelor of Applied Science, majoring in turf management, and he'd wanted to travel a little more before settling into his career back home.

In July that year our family had travelled to England for a family wedding — our brother Guy was marrying Melanie. Marky and I had flown out of Auckland at similar times but on different airlines, as he was going on to America. I recall seeing him off at the airport and having a heavy wave of sadness fall on me. I'm not normally emotional at goodbyes, so it was a very strange feeling — like I wasn't going to see him again. We met up a day or two later in London and went to the wedding. Once again, saying goodbye to him at Heathrow, I felt this sadness and I just couldn't get away from it.

That was the last time I would see him.

Nothing I'd ever gone through in my life had prepared me for this. At first I just sat there in a bit of a daze, thinking, What the . . .? What's going on? What does this mean? It was a surreal experience because Mark was on the other side of the world, in Mexico as it turned out, and here we were being told the chopper was missing. I felt dumbfounded, and in denial: 'Don't be ridiculous. Of course you can find them.' How hard is it to locate a helicopter?

Then 45 minutes later we got another call from James telling us the dreadful news. They'd found the crash site, and no one had survived. Three New Zealanders were killed on impact: Mark, James's son Dan, and the pilot, Adam Trevor. My whole world collapsed. I thought, Where do we go from here? What do we do? So many things were going through my mind — the shock of it, denial, disbelief, hate, sadness, blame — all these emotions washed over me in a big wave.

But it wasn't only about me. There were three of us in the kitchen at Te Parae at that moment, trying to take in this information. When I looked at Mum and Dad and saw the sadness in their eyes I realised there was nothing I could do about it, and that was terrible, that feeling of helplessness. All we could do was sit there, the three of us, and hug each other, almost holding each other up in complete shock: Mum and Dad trying to take in that they'd lost a son and me my twin brother.

We were great mates, Marky and I. I was the treasured only daughter, of course, but he understood that. As little toddlers, when Dad was bathing us, he used to joke, 'Just let the plug out and the others can go down with the bathwater, so long as you catch her.' Marky had always been gorgeous to me. We used to have a swing under the oak tree on the lawn and he always let me go first. When we stayed with Granny Phelps, Mum's mother, and helped with the baking, he would always offer me the mixing bowl to scrape clean. He was lovely like that. Even with his huge collection of Smurfs — if I wanted to play with them, he never fought with me about it. He never seemed to mind that his twin sister was the first precious Williams girl. And now he was gone.

Even when I talk about it now it's hard to find words to express how I felt. Certainly there's no book to explain how you navigate your way through all those immediate reactions; how you should deal with everything. I guess we must have sat there for a good hour. Looking back, it's amazing how you just box on when your morning has been absolutely blindsided by two dreadful phone calls.

***

The company Mark was working for, Helicopter Wildlife Management, was owned and run by New Zealander James Innes and based in Salt Lake City, Utah. Tim had been working for them for a while but he had come home for Christmas while Mark stayed on.

Most of their work was adventure-related, working for the American equivalent of the Department of Conservation. They specialised in the live capture of deer, moose, bear — similar to the typical Kiwi outback work. On that fateful day, they were live-netting bighorn sheep on Tiburón Island in Mexico, which is situated about 15 kilometres off the coast in the Gulf of California. Mark's job was in the back of the chopper. There was the pilot; the shooter in the front, who would fire the net gun over the sheep; and Mark, who would jump out of the chopper, lasso the sheep and hook it under the chopper. This particular morning, the boys had just fuelled up and were out on their first run when the chopper hit the side of a hill and exploded on impact. Tiburón Island is considered among the most difficult capture sites in the world, but the boys knew what they were doing; they weren't cowboys. The previous day they'd taken 34 sheep out of there. It's extremely rugged terrain, with sheer rock faces; it's sparsely populated, but quite a special area for reptiles and wildlife.

As a mark of respect to them and their work, the North American Wild Sheep Conference set up an 'In Memoriam' webpage to the three boys, with a photo taken on the morning of the crash of Dan Innes releasing a bighorn ram, and Adam Trevor in the background, piloting a helicopter; the caption states that Mark was still back on the mainland when the photo was taken. The tributes to the three demonstrate the high regard in which they were held among their American colleagues. Dan is described as an 'outstanding netgunner and animal handler . . . through his efforts over 600 bighorn were radio-collared for research, tested for disease, and restored to historic habitat'. Adam, 26, only recently arrived from New Zealand, with 5000 hours of flying time, was 'highly regarded by his comrades and countrymen'. And, of course, our Marky: 'bright, talented, a promising career ahead of him, a veteran netgunner and animal handler, Mark wanted the experience of capture work and he quickly became a natural with the animals.'

***

We couldn't sit in the kitchen crying forever — not even for the rest of the day. The Williamses have a strong practical streak; we come from a long tradition of doing what needs to be done. As distraught as Mum and Dad were, there were things that needed to be seen to. First we had to get hold of Guy and Tim and break the bad news to them. Guy was a stock agent at the time, and he'd gone to a sale at a local bull stud, while Tim was out enjoying a day's fishing. Dad didn't tell them over the phone; he waited until they came home.

When I write this and recall their faces, and the look in their eyes . . . it's heartbreaking to watch someone's life crumble. It is something you never get over.

Tim had to get away from Te Parae for a while because he felt so guilty. He said Mark was doing the job he should have stayed behind to do, and it should have been him in the chopper. Dad had actually told Mark to come home for Christmas, but Mark had wanted to work over that period. When he made the decision to stay in America, Tim said to him, 'Don't go down to Mexico because you'll get rolled, bowled and arseholed down there.' Timmy's the practical person. He can survive pretty much anything. If you get stranded on an island you want to be with Tim, because he'll guarantee you'll survive. I think he was also feeling frustrated because he'd told Mark not to go there, but Mark had felt obliged to fit in as much work for the company as he could. He'd been staying with them, travelling around the United States, and he really wanted to work.

So here we were, just before Christmas, thrown into this tumultuous time. Of course it hit the news in New Zealand: three Kiwi boys killed in a helicopter crash in Mexico. It didn't help that there were rumours of sabotage — the *New Zealand Herald* ran a story about 'skulduggery' in Mexico and 'suspected sabotage' — but fortunately that turned out to be false: the Ministry of Foreign Affairs in Wellington said it 'had heard nothing to suggest foul play'. That didn't stop the phones ringing and by the end of the day people were asking, 'What's going on? Is this true? Oh my goodness.' But this is a lovely community here, and the offers of help soon started flooding in; everyone was so kind and incredibly supportive.

In the midst of all this turmoil, by that afternoon we had to start thinking through all the logistics of bringing Marky home. Tim said, 'Well, I'm definitely going back because it's my job. I know the systems, I know how everything works and I know everyone in the company.' And I chimed in, 'I'm not going to stay round here and mope. I'm coming with you to bring the boys home.' I don't recall there was ever a question of my not going. Dad just said, 'If that's what you want to do, Mouse, you go.'

Then our friend Rico rang and said to me in his usual gruff voice, 'Rat!' (He's always called me Rat instead of Mouse.) 'Rat, I'll come to Mexico with you.'

For years our family had been very close friends with Richard 'Rico' Riddiford — founding chief executive of Palliser Wines in Martinborough and fifth-generation resident of the Wairarapa. Granny Phelps used to teach him at Sunday school when he was a very young chap. At the very start of Toast Martinborough, the annual food and wine festival in the Martinborough village, Mum and her friend Christina Buchanan would provide the catering for Palliser Wines via their company Sausage Rolls Inc., and in the summer holidays Marky and I would work on the Palliser vineyard. Rico would also get us to do odd jobs around his big historic homestead, Tablelands: cleaning gutters, mowing lawns, babysitting his nephews and nieces, anything he could think of really. And now he was offering to come with us to Mexico.

'No, Rico,' I told him. 'That's very kind of you, but Timmy and I will be okay. We'll get it sorted.'

'No you bloody won't. I'm removed enough from the family. I'll sort it out.'

I had no energy to argue with him. It's a waste of time trying to argue with Rico anyway. And he was absolutely incredible, simply a saviour. For instance, he was friends with Rod Deane, then head of Telecom, and when we flew out of Wellington Rod and his wife Gillian were at the airport with a stack of cellphones for us to take that would operate in the US, in Mexico, wherever we went. Today we'd take it for granted, but back then cellphones weren't so available, and we weren't as reliant on them. Gillian would phone us every day to check on us, see how we were. I had never met this couple before, and found them to be the most generous people, with us in spirit every day while we were over there.

We had no idea what we were heading into. I can't remember what I packed to take with me; my state of mind went completely out the door. My passport and maybe one change of clothes and that was it, because I ended up buying clothes over there. I was obviously slightly naïve about how long it would take to get the boys released — Mexico was not New Zealand, in terms of processing through bureaucracy. We were in the dark; all we really could focus on was that the boys were still in Mexico.

We flew to Los Angeles then to Hermosillo, an industrial city and the capital of Sonora state in Mexico, which was the closest city to where the boys were taken when they were recovered from the crash site. I felt totally exhausted even before take-off, and the trip seemed to take forever: we had to get to Los Angeles, change planes and fly on to Mexico. However, no sooner had we landed in Hermosillo than I was told I needed to go immediately to identify the boys. This was such a shock, and I must admit that at this stage my courage started to falter. I balked at that. 'I need to backtrack a bit,' I said to Rico. 'I don't think I can do this.'

In the end, Tim identified all three, and Rico and I entered the morgue and identified Marky along with Tim.

It was tough. I only identified Marky; I didn't see the other boys. I never thought that at 25 years of age I'd be signing my brother's death certificate.

It was Christmas Eve and we were sitting there stuck for what seemed like ages in this concrete bunker. Even though the sun was shining, it was a chilly day. Then, when we walked down the concrete steps below ground into the bunker, my eyes took that extra second to adjust. It was cold and damp. We watched a middle-aged Mexican woman who looked like she'd never seen an ounce of makeup in her entire life and had a headscarf holding back her wispy black hair, crouch over a small school desk just big enough for her typewriter, taking ages to type out the death certificate with one finger. We then had to choose urns for the boys' ashes, which involved walking into a room with shelves that went on and on. This was an experience that seemed so surreal — in what universe would you ever imagine you might be shopping for urns?

After what seemed like an eternity, it was over. We had the boys' ashes in our care. We could bring them home.

When we left Hermosillo airport with the ashes, the security team told me they remembered Mark coming into the country, and passing through security on his way into the city. Maybe it was because he was bringing in helicopter parts and nets for animal recovery — who knows? But even they were aware of the accident and they passed on their respect to us and the families of the two other boys.

***

Despite the journey being so grim, there was the odd funny moment. One that sticks in my mind was when we were flying from LA to Hermosillo on some dodgy Mexican airline and I thought, 'God, this is just what Mum and Dad need, to lose two more children in this crappy old plane.' I swear I looked back down the aisle and saw chickens in cages — that kind of scenario.

Rico was sitting next to a Mexican man. It was early evening and the man kept turning off Rico's light because he wanted to sleep but Rico kept turning it back on again. It went on and on until Rico was so over it, he snapped, 'Fuck off, gringo.'

I said, 'No, Rico, we're the gringos. Don't say that!' It was just so stupid, and it made us all giggle.

On the way home from Mexico we were stuck in Hermosillo airport trying to get back to LA and we realised it was Christmas Day. We thought we'd better do the right thing and scout around for something to eat, to at least acknowledge it was a Christmas dinner. Well, guess what our Christmas Dinner was? A skody piece of pizza. We got the giggles because we thought, Hell, here we are, sitting in this foreign country surrounded by these three urns and our Christmas dinner is a piece of four-day-old pizza. There was nothing we could do but laugh about it because we'd just been through this emotional roller coaster — getting to the boys, identifying them, signing the death certificates, and then getting them through customs. What a nightmare.

I had to deal with all these things so unexpectedly. A week before I had been sailing through life without a care, and now I was battling with Mexican bureaucrats to bring my brother home for his Te Parae funeral. I grew up so quickly in those few days.

One thing I will never forget is arriving at LA airport and seeing the koru symbol on the tail of the Air New Zealand plane. When you are feeling so far from home, and so miserable, something that simple can be so uplifting. It's such a relief and makes you realise, I'm nearly home. I'm nearly home.

We flew in to Wellington, where we were ushered through security by the very considerate and understanding Air New Zealand staff. Mum and Dad met us and took me back to Te Parae with Marky. Timmy flew on down to the South Island to take the other two boys home to their parents; Adam was from Greymouth and Dan was from Wanaka. Tim stayed a night with each family, talking to them about what we'd done, trying to give them some clarity, before coming back to Te Parae for the funeral, which Mum, Dad and Guy had been planning while we'd been in Mexico.

I never met the Trevor family, even though we talked regularly when I was in Mexico and when I got back home. When Tim returned from taking Adam back to them on the West Coast he gave me a small piece of kyanite, a gift to me from Mick Collins, a jade carver who lived on the West Coast. None of us had met him but he had heard about the death of the boys and had carved three pieces from kyanite — one for Dan's mother Bim Innes, one for Adam Trevor's sister, and one for me. An aluminium silicate, blue kyanite is very rare but is found in the Jacobs River in South Westland, and is a heeling stone that apparently carries the essence of divine feminine energy and provides a calming effect. I was told this particular stone can only be given to females. The gift was an act of kindness with enormous meaning, which will always remain with me.

We held the whole funeral service on the front lawn on 6 January 1999. It was a lovely day, screaming hot, but as most people who've been through the same thing probably agree, it all remains a bit of a blur. Mum's cousin Tony Phelps played the organ; our family friend and Anglican minister Warner Wilder took the service; and eulogies were read by Marky's girlfriend Sarah McOviney, his good mate Mike Ussher, his tutor from Massey University Martin Wrigley, and of course Rico. I do remember there was a massive amount of support from everyone who turned up for the funeral, young and old.

One particular memory that certainly added to the day occurred after the ceremony. My parents asked me to look in the washhouse. My first response was, 'I'm trying to get through our saddest day and you want me to go to the washhouse?' At that moment I did think my parents had finally taken leave of their senses. But off I went — to find this little black ball of fur, which came out wagging its tail. A black Labrador puppy. She was a present from the Chittick family and had been brought down that day to Te Parae by Garry and Mary Chittick from Waikato Stud in Matamata. The pup was related to Bear, Rico Riddiford's infamous Labrador, and because she was given to me at Mark's funeral I named her Sparkle Bear, a combination of Mark's nickname Sparkle and Bear.

I then found out why Garry had turned up at the funeral not dressed in his usual polished manner. On the trip down from the Waikato the puppy had had a mishap over him, making a mess of his suit. When they arrived in Masterton they made a mad dash to Susie and Buzz's place and, much to Garry's disappointment, had had to find a new outfit from my uncle's wardrobe.

Sparkle Bear lived a long and happy life at Te Parae until she died in 2012. The Big Room now holds a lovely portrait of her, painted by the artist Anna Guild.

***

No parent should have to bury their children. I doubt Mum and Dad will ever get over it. I certainly don't believe in closure, if that means shutting the book on something. There was a report done on the helicopter crash but I never read it because, for me, that wasn't going to change anything. Mark's gone, and Adam and Dan who were with him are gone, and that's that. But I totally appreciate why families want to visit the site where their loved ones died. Even though we couldn't go to the actual crash site, we visited the beach at Hermosillo and looked across the bay towards the hill country where the boys lost their lives. I'm trying hard not to sound clichéd, but to be in the vicinity was a moment of, 'This is it, the finality. This is the place on earth that Mark was last alive. Done. Now let's get the boys home.'

Then you do have to move on and enjoy life again. The generosity of friends and extended family was and is overwhelming. I hope no one ever has to go through such a situation, but, if you do, know that everyone around you is there to help. It's impossible to get through tragedy on your own; no one person can be that much of a martyr. In some families, among the children, there is one who stands out as the strong one, who takes over and manages all the arrangements; but when I think about Guy, Tim and me in our situation, we all became strong, even though each one of us dealt with the tragedy in different ways. This is most likely because both our parents were incredibly strong, and they led by example. The more I look back, the more I can appreciate their resilience — how welcoming they were to all and sundry who arrived to share their grief. They were strong for anyone who walked through the door of Te Parae, when I know that all they really wanted to do was shut up shop and hibernate. They were determined not to let this beat them.

When I was interviewed for a feature for *Life & Leisure* magazine, writer Sharon Stephenson described me, à propos of Mark's accident, as someone who 'elbows aside the dark clouds and goes straight for the silver lining'. That's true. I told her at the time that 'Mark was such an outgoing person who embraced life. He really taught me to put myself out there'. But it's also part of the makeup of our family, both present and past generations; part of our gene pool, I guess. It was as if we said, 'This is the situation, so let's deal with it.' Even in the midst of our tragedy Dad still managed to tell the newspapers that Marky was doing what he'd always been encouraged to do from the time he was a kid — seize any chances that came his way. 'I have tried to instil in all my kids that opportunities present themselves relatively infrequently and you should take them,' he said to the *Herald*. 'He was an adventurous sort of soul.'

And we've all done that — seized our chances. You have to live with your life; you can't stop taking risks. Tim now owns and runs Wairarapa Helicopters Limited and every day his partner, Haley Mills, sees him go out flying. Mum hears his chopper go overhead and I've heard her comment that her heart's in her mouth, and she breathes a sigh of relief when she hears it fly home at the end of the day. That must be hard for her, losing a son in a helicopter accident and then having another son who does it for a living. I admire her for the way she manages that; it's a very tough situation for a mother.

Guy is now married to Kim, and farms the largest block of Te Parae Station. Of course there are always potential hazards on farms, but there are dangers in everyday life. I work around horses all the time; I'm chainsawing trees by myself or doing all manner of rough stuff maintaining the homestead while Simon is away at work. Accidents happen in those situations. But Mark would be the last person to expect us to stop enjoying our lives to the full. Both Guy and Tim have children and we talk to them a lot about Uncle Marky because we want the nephews and nieces to know they had another uncle. It's very important for them that we keep his memory alive.

***

For families who've lost a loved one, anniversaries are hard times: the pain and the sadness come flooding back. For us, Mark's anniversary is always at Christmas, when everyone is joyous and celebrating. But, strange as it may seem, we've never made that a depressing time for the family. We talk to each other and say, 'This is for Marky.' We don't make it sad. As time goes by you do recall the fond memories and that's what you hold on to.

Obviously there are down times, too. Whenever I feel sad I phone Tim, because he's a great leveller. He'll buck me up with a good talking to. 'Well, Mouse, no point in being sad. He's dead. You can't bring him back. You can't change it, so let's move forward.' And he's right. For sure, you do need to go through that mourning process, but there's no point in being sad all the time; you have to start talking about the funny times, too — like how we used to call Marky Rumpelstiltskin because he used to throw a wobbly really easily, and he'd get so mad he'd jump up and down on the same spot. When we talked about things like this — the lighter moments — it helped us through.

Don't get me wrong, there are still times I shed a tear for him. Being a twin, growing up together and having that special relationship . . . of course I do. When we were toddlers Mum says we had our own kind of language to communicate. I think about him a lot. We never really fought as little kids, only as teenagers, and the only serious fight I really recall was when he shot me with the slug gun. I was in the kayak and he said, 'Start rowing, Mouse.' The slug ricocheted off the water onto my arm — the pain! I told Mum and he was really dark about that. But mostly it was great. Growing up out here at Te Parae, even though there were always heaps of people coming and going, it was always cool to have a mate your own age. Every birthday I think of him, and I often wonder what he would have been doing now.

Six months after Mark died it was our graduation ceremony at Massey University. Knowing how long these things can go on for I was grateful it was the same ceremony for both of us as I went up and accepted Mark's qualification posthumously.

The Te Parae doorstep got a major workout after his death, with so many people visiting to share stories with us about their times with him. We were given many gifts in the form of plants — shrubs, roses, trees — I'm sure the local garden centres did a roaring trade. In the end, Mum and Dad cleared a two-acre section of bush to the west of the house and planted all this gorgeous flora. It's complemented by a memorial comprising a sculpture by Sarah McOviney inserted into a slab of totara. This area is called Marky's Garden and now plays a big part in wedding receptions.

Sometimes I dream of Mark. I'm talking to him, telling him that I haven't caught up with him in ages. 'Where have you been? I haven't seen you around.' I'll wake up, reality sets in and I realise he is no longer with us. We all miss him dreadfully, but that's the hand we've been dealt and we have no choice but to get on with it.

***

When Mark left school he completed an Outward Bound course at Anakiwa. On his solo experience he wrote this poem, which has been recited at just about every family wedding, and no doubt will also do the funeral rounds when those times come.

LIKE A FERN
Our lives are similar to that of a fern.
We start out small with so much to learn.
As time rolls on a fern will roll out,
Leaves will appear like adventures will do.
The first leaves that appear represent our first steps in life.
As time goes by more leaves will appear,
New adventures, experiences for us to all share.
Old memories are left far, far behind,
As we strive to reach forward in order to find,
New friends, experiences and people to love,
For without any of these our lives would be dull.
Eventually with time the weight of life gets too much,
Our bones become frail, we start to lose touch,
However, if it was not for our family and friends,
We may have given up hope or reason, it depends!
But always remember that just like a fern,
Our lives do have purpose from which we must learn,
To teach and tell the young ones about so they can discover
Their true worth without feeling discouraged or lonely,
Which no one enjoys,
For in this big world, although we are small,
We all count for something,
So go on, give it your all!
—Mark Williams

From then on I was determined to give life my all. No more mucking around in someone else's kitchen, taking orders from grumpy cooks. But first I had to get away again, lick my wounds and clear my head of the sorrows of losing my twin brother. I cleared the hell out of Masterton and across the Tasman.

Angela in Australia, June 2000.

CHAPTER FOURTEEN

Melbourne

There's nothing like retail to focus your thoughts. I found myself working in Toorak, a ritzy, upmarket suburb of Melbourne, in a bed-linen-cum-homewares store, and I stayed with close family friends Judi and David Rosback. In my silent grief — I've never been one to openly mourn — they became my Aussie parents.

I knew them well because their son Charles had worked at Te Parae some years earlier. Wherever we go in the world it seems there's always a place to stay with someone whose kids have worked in our stables or on the farm.

It was 1999 and I was 26. I had considered working in an Australian vet clinic but at my first job interview I saw a customer bring in an enormous tarantula to be cared for and that put me right off: I said no, thank you very much, and kissed goodbye to my career in vet nursing.

I soon become proficient in bed-linen thread counts, colour

coordination with sheet sets and duvet covers, ironing sheets on beds and even dressing the odd shopfront window. Again the old adage: you name it, I did it! I immersed myself in a Kiwi contingent playing touch rugby, and got back into the horse-racing scene; I even survived the full calendar week of the Melbourne Cup Carnival! That was a really tough time but the Rosback family were a tower of strength and helped me through it.

Working in retail proved to be a good learning curve in customer service, which again came back to help me later when staging events. I learned a very harsh lesson when a young mother came in with her baby in a pram and I thought all was well. She seemed polite and interesting — until I discovered the coffee machine had been stolen. When we looked back at the CCTV tape, wo found the guilty party: lady with pram! I'd forgotten what I learned in those pubs in Ireland in my gap year: don't assume anything about people just from their appearance.

I felt I needed a bit of focus. So I went on one of those tour trips from Uluru, through Kakadu National Park and up to Darwin. Travelling, camping and sightseeing with 15 strangers was liberating as I didn't have to explain who I was or what I had been through. It was a relief! We walked up Uluru, held all sorts of reptiles, swam with freshwater crocs, went four-wheel driving through the Kakadu and visited parts of Australia I never knew existed.

I also drove the Great Ocean Road from Melbourne to Adelaide with Susie Rosback, playing the ultimate tourists. When we reached Adelaide we stayed with family friends, the Haighs. Both Alister and Simon Haigh worked at Te Parae with the horses during the 1970s and now own and manage the well-known Haigh's Chocolates.

After realising the world carries on and does not stand still I felt emotionally strong again, my homing beacon switched on and I realised I needed to knuckle down and get serious about my career. It had been a good time out, staying with Mum and Dad's close friends, being treated as family, but it wasn't for ever. I loved Melbourne — it's a great city, with fabulous restaurants and cafés and an exciting social life. I couldn't bear to go back to quiet Masterton after that; I was only 27 years old, far too young to settle in the provinces. So I headed for Auckland. I thought I might try to get in the door of the racing industry. I could combine my love of working with horses with my passion for and knowledge of the industry. I didn't want to be a groom, but maybe I could work on the administration side of things then try to make my way up the ladder towards promotions and public relations. There was no point in approaching a rural racing club; 'I might as well go straight to the top and hound them until they give me a job,' I told myself firmly.

Easier said than done. For weeks I spent what seemed like every day annoying the marketing team at the Auckland Racing Club, badgering them to give me a job until, in the end, they gave in.

Finally I thought I had made it to the ideal job — working in marketing and promotion for the top racecourse in New Zealand, with the added bonus of seeing horses on race day, plus I didn't have to groom, preen or pamper the animals at ungodly hours of the morning 365 days a year. It didn't bother me at all that there would be racing every second Saturday — which meant going to work — or that I would be working crazy hours on a meagre wage. I had the best of both worlds: sitting in my office organising events around horses.

I spent many hours working on Fashions in the Field, which is a huge promotion during the racing calendar's premier week over the Christmas period. Racegoers enter a competition in which they parade their race-day outfits to win prizes. It's always amazingly popular, with fierce competition among the fashionista racegoers. There was inevitably the weird and outrageous: we would have some contestants wearing body paint and little else, others in fancy-dress costumes of papier-mâché horse and jockey, and then there were the serious haute-couture outfits that would not have looked out of place on the runways at Paris Fashion Week! To add some spice and enhance our event at Ellerslie, I spent a bit of time with the management team at Victoria Racing Club, Flemington, in Melbourne, picking their brains about their Fashions on the Field event. Every year we tried to improve and it always got more competitive. The judges never failed to be impressed with the rising standards — even though it made their task that much harder!

On race days my job was not as glamorous as those strutting their latest fashions, though; I was there to work. Without sponsors, there would be no races. I had to make sure the representative of the sponsor for each race was down in the birdcage to see their race and to celebrate with the winning owners and trainers of the horse, plus to gift any trophies associated with the race. That could be rather trying at times, attempting to interrupt and usher the sponsor away from their socialising — particularly from race seven onwards!

One particular occasion I went in to the Chairman's Room — which, tongue firmly in cheek, we called 'God's waiting room' because it is patronised mostly by elderly guests — looking for the sponsor in question. He was there, but deep in conversation with the Mayor of Auckland City at the time. I stood there politely trying to make eye contact with the sponsor. I could see the mayor looking at me so he then proceeded to puff out his chest and continue this long diatribe for what seemed like an eternity until he eventually stopped, looked at me again and said, 'I'm ready to come down to the birdcage now.' I politely replied, 'Oh, there's no need. I'm not here for you. I require this gentleman here, who is sponsoring the next race. If you would excuse us, we need to be in the birdcage for the race.' I'm sure the group of people around us would have been chuckling away inside, but they didn't dare show it.

A small part of my job was to source and order trophies and horse rugs for the premier days and, in particular, the Group One races. I would receive a budget that I was supposed to stick to but, naughtily, I never did. According to my thinking, if my horse could get into a Group One race on a premier race day then I would expect to receive a trophy with presence, one that I could be proud of and hopefully make use of — like all the silver jugs, trays and crystal glassware trophies won by my father, uncle and grandparents and used at Te Parae. I did argue each year to increase the budget but to no avail — although that never stopped me ploughing through the money before the season was finished.

One day I received a phone call from a trainer's wife before the Christmas Carnival — Auckland Racing Club's four days of racing, parties and fashion events over Christmas time. They had a horse in one race and she wanted to know what trophy I had chosen for the race in question, as she wanted it to match a trophy they had previously won. I felt a little uneasy about being told what to have as a trophy, and wasn't even sure that this was above board. But then I had a think about it and decided she had a point: if she had a chance to win a couple more Jasper Conran crystal wine glasses to make a full set, matching the previous trophy they had won, and she thought they had a good chance to do so, then why not ask? As it happened I did have the glasses as the trophy, and sure enough they won the race! So here's hoping that each time they use the glasses they thank the horse that won and the girl who went over budget to get the matching trophy.

On every single race day you will find so many people working hard behind the scenes, from tote staff, who place bets for punters, to trackside staff, who televise the races, and track managers making sure the track is capable of handling 10 races with about 100 horses galloping at full speed to bar staff catering for the hundreds wanting beers, wines and spirits all at the same time. Then there is the race-day management trying to ensure everything runs smoothly. Without these people, race days would never happen. It is a hive of activity. I would spend my time walking between stands to track down sponsors, organising photos of the winning horse and connections to the horse — owners, trainers, all delighting in the win — then ushering everyone into the winner's circle to celebrate, then manoeuvring everyone out so this procedure could be repeated another nine times with the next nine winners on the day. In flat shoes this would be a breeze; in heels . . . oh, my poor feet! It was a long day and by race 10 I was ready to see a podiatrist.

At Auckland Racing Club there were a few people who would always make my job that much easier, and with whom I really enjoyed working. The first was Norm Holland, an ex-jockey who was in charge of weighing-in the jockeys after each race. He also had to make sure the saddle blankets were gathered and accounted for and distributed for the next race; and he organised the jockeys to get to the mounting yard for the upcoming race. He would be in the birdcage ready to go well before race one. Norm always looked dapper in his neatly pressed suit, shirt and tie, and never failed to tip his felt hat to acknowledge me each race day. He constantly had a cheeky smile on his face and was ever ready to spin a good yarn about the 'old days in racing'; he even remembered my grandparents, Alister and Nancy.

The other gentleman was David in the winner's circle. This was his domain, and he'd be standing there in his smart outfit with his bow tie. He was so good at hosting the winning connections that it was almost impossible to ask them to leave before the next group head in! David was always ready to remind me where I was going next, what race we had coming up, and generally be my time keeper.

I can't forget Sonya Anderson, who was in charge of sponsorship, and helped me keep my sanity when chasing sponsors' reps all over the complex! She is a very accomplished networker who had a great memory for trainers, racegoers and sponsors. She was an encyclopedia of names and faces!

One of the great characters in the racing game was Keith Haub, race caller at the Ellerslie Racecourse and for the upper North Island. He also owned the very good horse McGinty. One time Hauby, as he was known, was calling a maiden race that my mare WaitAMinute happened to be running in during the Auckland Carnival. She won the race (I promise this wasn't rigged) and, in my wild excitement, I distinctly remember Hauby calling in the flow of his commentary, 'Nice to see the old Te Parae colours back in the winner's circle. No doubt Miss Williams will enjoy the win!'

Such a proud moment — and such a great job; after three years in the marketing team I thought this was the perfect place for me. Then the past chairman of the Auckland Racing Club, Barry Neville White, approached me and suggested I apply for a job that was available in Auckland at Louis Vuitton New Zealand. I think I looked at him a little blankly. I thought, I'm perfectly happy here, working at the Racing Club. Do I need to move? Will this be of benefit to me? I must admit I knew very little about Louis Vuitton, let alone how the brand was represented in New Zealand. I was one of those Kiwis who assumed Louis Vuitton was something to do with sailing. But then it seemed like a challenge; should I just see how far I could get through the interviews? Barry and his wife Deirdre were very supportive of me and encouraged me to make the move.

Once I started the process, the excitement grew, and when I learned more about the company I couldn't wait to get there. Suddenly I was packing up my desk at the Auckland Racing Club and moving into my new office at the bottom of Queen Street. It was such a big change in culture, going across town from the world of horse racing to promoting one of the universe's leading fashion labels. I sometimes had to pinch myself — how did this shy mouse from rural Wairarapa make the change from jodhpur boots and saddles to stilettos and fancy handbags?

Once more, I took the skills I had learned at the Racing Club with me to Louis Vuitton, built on them, and used them to the max when organising the parties I've written about. And when I left that job seven years later and fetched up back at Te Parae, ready to run my own business, I could draw on my whole career experience: starting with the lowest of jobs overseas making kedgeree at five in the morning, cooking for skiers in Queenstown, carting trayloads of hot muffins over planks on sawhorses, schmoozing the sponsors and vamping fashions at Auckland Racing's Cup Week, and culminating in coordinating the ultimate Vuitton events. No job I'd done in hospitality or marketing had gone to waste.

Te Parae homestead today.

CHAPTER FIFTEEN

Where to start?

We had arrived at Te Parae, and now we were ready to create a new website, open the doors to paying guests, plan events and weddings, build up a base of reliable photographers, caterers, hire centres, nearby accommodation places — the conglomeration of things we would need to operate a successful business here.

A police officer and me — someone you might call a Jill-of-all-marketing-and-cooking-trades. Once the initial euphoria of the move had worn off, it hit me what a truly enormous change we'd made in our lives. Every morning Simon would go off to work at the Masterton Police while I stayed home and got stuck into fixing up the old place. Mum and Dad were there to help, but I had totally underestimated how hard I was going to have to work and just how much there was to do.

I know Simon sometimes found it difficult, at the age of 40, to be living under the same roof as his parents-in-law, but in reality there was no way I could have managed on my own without them in that first year. They had been in our position themselves, as young not-so-newly-weds, and they were well acquainted with the way in which the grounds could get away from you if you turned your back for just one week in the springtime. One week of warm weather and gentle rains in October and November and next thing the weeds would be towering over the flowerbeds, laughing at you. Dad could tell me where the prevailing winds came from, and Mum could point out what plants and shrubs were best suited to which areas — all that invaluable historic knowledge that saves time and money.

They had built up so many invaluable friends and contacts, too; they are well known throughout the Wairarapa and beyond. But that's not the only reason I'm so proud of them. Some people might find it unusual for a woman my age, happily married and building her own life, to be so close to her parents, but mine are part of everything I do. Even when I was in Auckland I would phone them four or five times a week to find out how the horses and dogs were getting on, or to ask if they'd bred any pigs yet. I wanted to know everything that was happening on the farm. Had Mum been to Wellington to buy new clothes? What parties or lunches had they attended or held at Te Parae? Our lives are extremely interconnected. Take Wings Over Wairarapa, for instance — a three-day biennial event, held in January at Hood Aerodrome in Masterton (a regional airport that Dad had been involved in from the beginning). Because of Dad's huge passion for flying, in 1999 he had this big idea to hold an airshow on Wellington Anniversary Weekend — and when I say 'Dad had an idea' I mean 'Dad had an idea that the whole family would be involved in'. The cry went out: 'You kids have to come home from wherever you are and help.'

At the first event, we were ordered around as the unpaid staff. Mum and I did the catering, cutting and packing hundreds of aeroplane-shaped shortbreads and producing trays galore of muffins, bread rolls and cakes. I spent days on the quadbike shovelling gravel into potholes up the drive at Hood Aerodrome and helping measure out the Gold Pass (corporate and VIP) area; and I provided lunch for all staff. No matter how sleep-deprived we felt, the public had paid for tickets and they were coming. As soon as the gates opened, the onslaught began: people jostling for the best spot by the runway, getting the perfect shot of the World War II Spitfire or the Mustang, wanting to meet the pilots.

Liz Pollock, the event manager, and Dad took the show from humble beginnings to one of the leading airshows in New Zealand; from 10,000 people over two days to around 25,000 over three days.

Even when I was in Auckland working fulltime I would take two weeks' annual leave and come home to help. It was important to me to stay involved with this airshow. For one thing, we'd been virtually brought up out at that aerodrome when we were little, spending hours mucking around while Dad was in meetings or working on planes. And for another, it was for Mum and Dad's sake: they had worked so hard over the years on Wings, and by giving a little bit back to them, I could say thank you to them. I didn't want to let them down. If Mum and Dad said, 'Can you help with this?' I would drop everything and do it. I never hesitated. They have never let us down, and I certainly don't ever want to let them down.

Of course another reason I helped out at the airshow was that I got to fly back to Auckland in a P51 Mustang, thanks to owner and pilot Graham Bethall, who lived in Auckland and housed the plane at Ardmore. Flying in one of these planes should be on everyone's bucket list. It's staggering to think young men were put in charge of these super-powered aircraft during World War II.

Boy did I rely on my parents when I started hosting my own events at Te Parae — and not just in terms of Mum's recipes. Fortunately by the time Simon and I returned to Te Parae, disastrous catering commissions like my début at Wimbledon were distant bad memories. I could now chuck several balls in the air and keep them up without the lot crashing to the floor in pieces. It was time to pull all the threads together from my peripatetic career and focus on Te Parae. But we couldn't do it on our own; we needed experienced staff. Who better than Tom and Gay? They had welcomed and catered for many people over the years at Te Parae. Their guests came from all over the world, and, because Dad was chairman of the Game Industry Board, promoting the Cervena venison brand, many of them were VIPs. If the walls of our homestead could speak, they'd tell you about a huge variety of wonderful lunches, parties and formal events Mum had orchestrated: the Korean delegation for the Game Industry Board, a group of Kuwaiti merchant bankers, Japanese groups for ICI, and many local companies holding their Christmas parties there.

On one of Sir Bernard Fergusson's official visits as governor-general to Te Parae, Buzz and Dad helped the aide-de-camp carry the luggage into the house. When Dad picked up a large black briefcase, Sir Bernard warned him, 'Be careful, Tom. Those are *the* state papers!' Dad took him seriously: he took the case into the house and gently placed it on the hall box. The governor-general then opened the briefcase, produced a bottle of gin, some glasses and a bottle of tonic, and proceeded to pour everyone a G&T! He commented to Mum that he called the briefcase his 'Justin Case'.

There are many other interesting names scattered throughout the Te Parae visitor books, reflecting the diverse range of people who have passed through these doors. Former governor-general Sir Willoughby Norrie visited in 1964; along with Granny Andy, he owned and raced a great jumper called Western Desert, and we still have a couple of Western Desert's trophies dotted throughout the homestead. William Whitelaw visited in the mid 1970s, as a guest of the New Zealand government; known as Willie Whitelaw, he was a Cabinet minister in the British Conservative government and leader of the House of Lords. At one stage he was deputy prime minister under Margaret Thatcher, giving rise to her famous quote, 'Every prime minister needs a Willie.' The names in the visitor books go on and on, and keep readers amused for hours.

Mum took her passion for cooking and entertaining beyond Te Parae for a while with her catering business. One of their biggest challenges was catering for the trade day before Toast Martinborough during its halcyon days — for the winemakers, chefs, judges and owners at Richard Riddiford's historic Tablelands property, a few kilometres out of Martinborough. Mum's propensity for hoarding has paid off: recently we came across one of her *My Recipes* books and found her preparations for this function. Between bursts of the giggles at some of the weird and quaint recipes she's gathered up over the years, we found this meticulous, professional-looking menu, including the 'Union Jack of Martinborough' and her note-to-self at the end:

APPETISER
Selection of Mini Sandwiches

SOUP
Chilled Avocado and Tomato served with Crostini

FROM THE SEA
Paua Fritters
Mussel and Prawn Platter

Hot Smoked Salmon in Pasta and Capsicum Salad with Lime and Dill Mayonnaise
Smoked Hoki and Stilton Tart

FROM THE LAND
Cervena with Fresh Herbs and Spices
Layered Pork and Chicken Terrine
Honeyed Ham on the Bone with Mustard and Mustard Fruits
Barbecued Cocktail Venison Sausages with Spicy Fruit Sauce
Hot Smoked Venison with Melon and Pawpaw
Black Forest Salami
Nelson Venison Salami

FROM THE GARDEN
Fresh Wairarapa Asparagus with Cucumber and Lime Sauce
Salad Medley of Organic Garden Greens

BAKERY
Fresh Baked Breads

DESSERT
Baba au Rhum with Seasonal Fruits

CHEESES
Puhoi Valley Brie
Aorangi Brie
Kikorangi Gorgonzola
Old Meyers Tasty Gouda
Dried Fruit and Nuts

COFFEE
Freshly Brewed Zorba/Mocha Mix

TEAS
Blended Herbal, Earl Grey, English Breakfast

PETIT FOURS
Selection

BON APPÉTIT!

SATURDAY 19 NOVEMBER 1994
TABLELANDS

Martinborough town laid out in shape of Union Jack. Tables were the same. Front of house — Blue Carpet.
Square in centre. ½ wine barrels, very large square umbrella.
Tables covered in white cloth with red strip down the middle.
Paper plates in red and white.
Serviettes in red, white and blue.
Excellent way to serve a large number of people.
Access to all tables.
Weather — only problem.

Mum has recorded everything in this recipe book: Guy and Sam's fifth birthday party menu, Tim's fourth birthday party, Mark's and my seventh birthday party in July for 50 kids. Every detail is there, from menus to set-up to guest lists — even the invitations. It's a resource I might well chuckle over, but it turned out to be a lifesaver when I started catering for big crowds myself at Te Parae.

When we started off with our first functions, Mum and Dad were my unpaid staff. It was perfect: they're old hands at it, and are so worldly, literally — they've travelled the world presenting Cervena to all different nationalities, and they can relate to all generations and all kinds of people.

Three years after we moved to Te Parae Simon left the police force when he was shoulder-tapped for a position as a racing investigator; that is, someone who checks out any corruption, drugging or dodgy business across all racing codes — harness, gallops and greyhounds. He'd always sworn he'd be a lifetime cop, but as he himself said, 'When I read the job application, I couldn't have written a better job description for myself if I'd tried.'

It's worked out well because most Saturdays and weekends, when we hold weddings and events, he's off at the races, and this means he has the whole week to ensure the gardens are all good to go.

The first couple of summers when I was doing all the functions on my own without hired staff, as inexpensively as I could, so that I could get my name out there and become known, Dad would be the barman and Mum the waitress. Simon and I would be hosting a bit but then there might be some drama going on out the back that we'd have to cope with — say, the meat was ready but the potatoes weren't — so I'd tell Mum and Dad to get out there and do whatever they needed to do to keep the guests amused. They would say, 'Of course, we can do that.' They would circulate, make conversation, put people at ease, and nobody would think anything was amiss.

My parents guide my life, and my business decisions. I'm so proud of them.

Angela's parents, Tom and Gay Williams, on their wedding day, 1968.

CHAPTER SIXTEEN

Miss New Zealand and Biggles

It's not as if we were indulged as children — on the contrary, our parents were quite strict and we obeyed them without arguing. We were never smacked, though Mum broke quite a few wooden spoons over the old kitchen table.

I remember Timmy stretched the boundaries left, right and centre; it was interesting to watch how he pushed Mum and Dad's buttons. But I remember Mum and Dad always being fantastic parents whom we respected. And if they said jump we asked how high. Once, when they were away during duck-shooting season, the boys decided to shoot up the main lake, which was totally not allowed — it had been a sanctuary since it was made. Mum and Dad came home early, heard all these shots being fired, and when the old man came around the side of the house they took one look at his face, dropped their guns and bolted!

Dad says Williams men have to marry amazing women because whoever they wed has to come back and make their home at Te Parae. Unlike brides who go off with their new husbands to build a dream home or buy a new house, then get to move into a new place with their own furniture and decorate in their own style, the Williams wives — at least the ones who married great-grandfather Guy, grandfather Alister and Dad — have had to move into Te Parae Homestead. A preference for old houses is certainly an advantage; and a love of the antiques, family heirlooms, fine silverware, trophy stags' heads mounted on the walls, racing awards, thoroughbred trophies and all sorts of other Williams paraphernalia that have collected over the past century is also important.

Luckily for Dad, Gay Loraine Phelps, the woman he set his eye on in the mid-1960s, really was amazing. If that name rings a bell with people Mum's age it's because she was Miss New Zealand in 1965 and went on to represent the country at the Miss Universe competition in Florida and the Miss World competition in London. She was brought up on a farm called Wainui on Moiki Road just out of Martinborough, went to Solway College in Masterton, then on to Auckland University. She and Dad met when she'd come home from Auckland for a spell to help one of her two sisters, Joy, whose two-year-old daughter Ondy had undergone a hip operation. Dad was taking the other sister, Carol, on a date. He walked into the house and saw Mum sitting on the couch with this young toddler on her knee and thought, 'She looks quite tidy.'

He didn't get a chance to have anything more to do with Mum at that time because she went back to Auckland, transferred to Teachers' Training College, and next thing she was off overseas representing the country as Miss New Zealand. When you look at these sort of pageants today, it's hard to imagine Mum even entering, because she's so modest. She was persuaded by Auckland friends who were budding lawyers and accountants associated with the Junior Chamber of Commerce to enter a Miss Personality contest to raise funds for the first Auckland rescue helicopter. She says she didn't read the fine print — typical — which automatically sent the first three winners through to the Miss Auckland competition.

Dad would have really thought he'd missed his chance when he picked up the 21 July 1965 copy of the *Weekly News* — a very popular large-format news magazine in those days — and saw a huge colour photograph of the 'quite tidy' sister looking extremely glam in a red wool ensemble with white fur collar, diamante drop earrings and matching brooch, and the big cover line: 'Gay Phelps: Our Candidate for Miss World and Miss Universe'.

Mum was reluctant. 'I hadn't wanted to go. When I found there were three of us left for the Miss Auckland competition I said, "I'm not staying." I was going to pull out. Then I saw one of the prizes was a black-and-white television set and I thought, Oh, we need one of those for the flat. It would be good to win a television set. It seems funny when you look back that I was persuaded by a television set.'

It's amusing to read about the way Miss New Zealand was described by the media back in July 1965, just before Mum headed off to the Miss Universe contest in Miami, Florida.

> Elegance and natural grace, both of appearance and manner, are among the most striking attributes the beautiful girl who is now representing the Dominion at that most glamourous — and gruelling — of the world's beauty contests . . . Gay Phelps, 21-year-old training-college student from Auckland, is a tall, slender girl — height 5 feet 8 inches, vital statistics 36–24–36. She is a true brunette with big, sparkling dark eyes, raven hair and a fine, creamy complexion. She has perfect teeth and very beautiful hands.

The article went on to describe Mum's upbringing in Wairarapa: her sisters — 'she is the middle one of three, all of whom have delightfully happy names' (Joy, Gay, Carol) — and her talent as a pianist and a singer — 'She had singing lessons for a time from Auckland's celebrated teacher, Sister Mary Leo. She is also an excellent performer on the piano accordion, which she first learned to play when she was 11 years old.' And, as if that weren't enough, Mum said she played cricket as a member of the teachers' college team, badminton, liked sewing, and 'especially loves cooking'. There were two black-and-white photographs of her: one playing the piano accordion, looking very serious, and the other posing in a suit, with a fluffy white handbag and white gloves.

Mum always insists she really enjoyed her time as Miss New Zealand because part of the job entailed visiting hospitals, doing store parades, appearing at all sorts of places where entrants don't go to now because the competition for entertainment is so much keener. 'It was great fun even though it was hard work,' she says. 'We travelled with entertainers like Howard Morrison, John Hore, Eddie Low and Peter Posa, and Joe Brown [the organiser] was such an interesting man — he was like an old grandfather. Dennis, his son, looked after me and he was a lovely man too. They paid me for two years — in 1966 when I was Miss New Zealand, and in 1967 as chaperone to the Miss New Zealand contestants — because I had to give up my teaching job. I did go back to teaching when that was over, two years later, and I was happy to go back.'

Mum hasn't changed much at all from that *Weekly News* cover girl. She has aged a bit, of course — it's 51 years since those photos were taken — and she's since raised four boisterous children, worked hard at Te Parae, endured deep sadness in her life, and supported my father's entrepreneurial streak, but she still looks as elegant and graceful as she was described in that somewhat cheesy article.

Mum would hate anyone saying that to her, though. She's so down-to-earth. She was brought up to dress beautifully by her mother, Gwen Phelps (née Garrity), who was the same; Granny Phelps made all her own clothes out of gorgeous silks and lovely fabrics. I remember Granny telling me that, when she was growing up in her large family of seven children during the Depression, all girls were taught to sew properly. Granny's own mother always looked smart, too, even though she was frantically busy with all those children and her husband away at war. Granny Phelps worked as a seamstress: she would go and stay with people in their homesteads, and sew all their clothes — men's shirts, women's dresses, beautiful children's clothes, anything her customers wanted. I have two of Granny's dresses that I have worn to functions like weddings and premier race days: both have a gorgeous silk lining and an outer layer of beautiful French lace. They are dresses I will always treasure, not only because they are vintage but because they were made and worn by my grandmother. Her sewing skills were passed down to two of her daughters, Joy and Carol, who both sew beautifully, including mastering the art of smocking, an embroidery technique used to gather fabric. Unfortunately that talent didn't quite make it to me!

Granny was of a generation that never left the house without a clean cotton handkerchief, and nor would she let any of her family go out without one. These days I'm not sure Gen-Y would even know what a handkerchief is, but Granny was famous in the Wairarapa for tucking a pretty hanky under her watchstrap. She was also well known for her special hanky made of vintage linen with delicate embroidery, which she would carry on special occasions. That hanky became part of her, in a way, and was passed around the family as a sort of beacon of strength in times of need. Granny gave it to me to take to Mexico when we went to bring Mark home. It seemed a natural thing to do at her funeral in 2010 to pass this special hanky around all and sundry to remember her by.

Thankfully, Mum returned to Masterton to teach at Hadlow after her Miss New Zealand stint and Dad caught up with her again. At that time it was Dad who was doing the entertaining at Te Parae, throwing these so-called 'bachelor parties' in the homestead. Lord knows how stylish they were compared to Mum's standards. He admits now, after much questioning, that the purpose of these parties was to find a wife. The invitations to the parties were quite classy, judging from one he's saved — printed in script on good-quality card:

At Home
Te Parae
Dancing at 9 pm
Dress Informal
20 February 1965

Sometimes he'd have a live band playing, and there might be beer and wine, though he says that in those days nobody drank much because they couldn't afford to have a car accident. 'The blokes drove FJ Holdens or Morris Minors, probably paid about £2500 for them, that they'd borrowed from the old man or from the farm.'

Dad seems to have been a bit of a Biggles character. Before he'd even gone for his driver's licence, he'd passed his pilot's licence, and in 1967 he bought a Tiger Moth. He'd been crazy about Tiger Moths since he was a kid at Hereworth School in Havelock North, when he used to go up Te Mata Peak on Sundays and take photos on his old Box Brownie of the Tiger Moths flying up the Tukituki River valley on a top-dressing run. 'They'd be spewing out fertiliser and I thought it was such a good sight. I took hundreds of photos. When I went to Wanganui Collegiate I told my father for my sixteenth birthday I wanted to learn to fly. He didn't want me to, but said if I could persuade the headmaster and housemaster to let me go to

Wanganui Aerodrome he'd consider it. I managed to do that, so my father paid the £120 for me to learn and I got my private licence, completed the forty or fifty hours and sat the test in Masterton.'

But, despite his confidence and derring-do, he nearly stuffed it up when he took Mum out for the first time. He was the most junior of junior stewards at the Masterton Racing Club at Opaki, and asked her to an evening function there. Because he was the lowest minion he had to tidy up afterwards. It was wintertime, a freezing-cold night, and, as he tells it, he'd parked his car in the middle of the racetrack and locked his keys inside. 'Here I was standing in the middle of the track in the middle of the night trying to impress this gorgeous girl and no keys.'

No problems, though, for this young farming chap. He took off his 'joddy boot', smashed the quarter-light window, unlocked the door and took her home. Mum *was* impressed: 'I thought, That's a strong and resourceful chap!'

Actually, they're both strong. Married in 1968, they have a good relationship. Dad has branched out into other areas, apart from regular sheep and cattle farming and the thoroughbred stud. There must have been times when Mum has raised her eyebrows, but she's always been there supporting him. For years he was involved in local politics — the then Masterton County Council — which for Mum meant more cooking and entertaining at Te Parae. They both enjoyed it, even though Mum jokes she never got the driveway tarsealed.

When we were children, Mum and Dad were away a lot of the time. Dad was on the Game Industry Board, chairing it for 10 years, and before that he was pioneering the capture of live deer from helicopters. Back in Masterton, Mum also put her time into the community: she was on the Drug and Alcohol Board in Masterton during the 1990s; and in 1988 she ran a Deer Farmers' Conference in Wellington, for which she created the event and organised a fashion display showcasing various outfits made of deer leather and suede, including jackets, suede skirts, slacks and even a pair of hotpants.

And of course Dad and Mum, along with Uncle Buzz and Aunt Susie, would always be off at the races, or over to Melbourne for the Cup Carnival. Dad was deeply involved with horse-racing administration, especially locally with the Masterton Racing Club. He was vice president of the New Zealand Thoroughbred Breeders' Association, and he became chairman of the Racing Authority, which took him all around the country. But being the bigwig didn't always mean he was in charge. One time when Dad was walking from the grandstand to the lunch area through the members' carpark at the Canterbury Jockey Club racecourse during their winter meeting, a lady he knew, Margaret Burnett, who had a determined stride and was wearing an enormous mink coat, grabbed him by the arm and said, 'You are coming to have a drink with me.' There was no way even my father could get out of that one. The official party continued on to lunch while Dad was frog-marched to Margaret's carpark space, where he was given a gin and a lecture on how to run racing. Margaret told him, 'You are a well-known stud breeder, you should lease fillies in the South Island.'

Dad knew he wasn't getting out of there without giving her a horse to race, and it so happened that he did have a three-year-old filly, by Sound Reason out of Riverlette, sitting at Te Parae, which he'd purchased from the Trentham yearling sales two years earlier from his good friend Gary Chittick. So to keep the peace he said to Margaret, 'I have this filly at home — you can have her.' Having completed the transaction, Dad quickly vacated the carpark and went to the official lunch.

There were 15 women in the carpark that day: each one of them took a share, and they named the filly Fifteen Reasons. Fifteen Reasons eventually made her way back to Te Parae and is the dam (mother) of my mare WaitAMinute.

The only other time, apart from at Te Parae, that I worked with Dad was when he was chairing the board of Seales — a company specialising in producing dairy cow and calf meal. I worked at the plant in Morrinsville for a short time. That was an experience, helping to bag feed then being sent out to farms around the Waikato district in my little white-and-yellow ute to deliver half a tonne of calf pellets in 20-kilogram bags to the cow cockies. I could see the eyes roll back in the heads of a few of the older farmers; I could almost read their lips. 'Oh God, a female . . . now I'm going to have to help her unload these bags.' It was a steep learning curve in diplomacy. I enjoyed listening to the old boys spin their yarns while I unloaded the bags of feed — usually by myself.

My brothers and I like to kid Dad about the things he's done, and he's always quick to crack a joke about himself. But in May 1997 our whole family took a trip to Government House in Wellington to watch proudly as Dad received an NZQSO (Companion of the Queen's Service Order) for his contribution to the deer and thoroughbred industry, and for his service to the community.

One of Mum's greatest talents — and I wish she had more time for it — is playing the piano. She gave piano lessons for the local school kids for about 15 years. I would often come home to find the kitchen littered with primary-school children munching their way through the best afternoon teas in the district. Friends have told me of fabulous parties at Te Parae where Mum sat down and played the piano, entertaining the guests. Sometimes I wish there were more hours in the day so she could just sit at the family piano in the dining room at Te Parae, surrounded by the old family portraits, and play to us while we relax in the cane chairs on the veranda, wine or beer in hand. In the future, maybe. For now, there are weddings to organise, lunches to plan and corporate retreats to finalise.

Angela's grandparents on her mother's side, Leo and Gwen Phelps, celebrating their 60th wedding anniversary in September 2000.

The dogs of Te Parae: Boo, Mukwa, Fin, Kevin, Max and Harry.

CHAPTER SEVENTEEN

Organised chaos

Sometimes I seriously doubt if I'll ever completely finish a task here. The day starts smoothly enough then suddenly everything turns crazy. And I'm not only talking about the weekdays; weekends are just as hectic. When winter starts to melt away into spring, that's when everything seems to burst into life.

It's such an enormous change from my life in Auckland, and even after five years it still hits me sometimes how different my life is now from the one I left behind, when I only worked five days a week and thought that was difficult. I think of it now when I'm in the garden at Te Parae, pulling out what seem like 10-foot-tall weeds from my 10-acre garden and ask myself, 'Why didn't I do this six months ago when it was a baby weed?' If I was back in Auckland I'd be doing something simple like going to the World fashion store up on Ponsonby Rd. My hands wouldn't be chapped and dry. My nails would be all nicely shaped and painted. I have tried shellac nails here on the farm but it doesn't work; they still break and tear. I am just not that Auckland person any more. I used to wake up on the weekends thinking, Mmmmm, what shall I do today? Here in the country there are not enough hours in my day to get everything done.

I only go up to Auckland now for horse sales. Yes, I might slip away for a quick look at Ponsonby Road, but I feel like a fish out of water. It's no longer my scene; I'm not that city girl at all. I feel really estranged from that life. But I still keep in touch with all those friends from The Stables and they come to stay at Te Parae, where we have a blast. They see our lifestyle in the summertime here, at the fun time — playing tennis, sitting around on the big verandas in the shade reading, snoozing under a shady tree, drinking gin and tonics with limes from our trees, boating on our big lake — and they think it's absolute bliss. They are really envious of what we have, though I do make them aware of how hard it is, all this work. A few of my Auckland friends — Jackie Shaw, Lydia Broadbelt, and Suze and Wayne Wheeler — have taken leave from their own jobs to come down and work for us at weddings as a favour. They say they love it even though I work them to the bone. I guess, because it is so different to what they are used to in Auckland, it's a novelty. Here they're among rural people; they feel they've come back to a farm, come home.

I like to feel it's my home, so it's their home, even if they wouldn't actually move permanently to live on a farm. Some of my girlfriends who were brought up on farms and are now married with children and live in Auckland come to stay, and the first thing they say is, 'I so miss not having our kids grow up with all this space.' They say it time and again. They would love their children to go to a country school as they did, and to have the room to run around, and ride ponies or motorbikes. You see this tinge of sadness that their kids won't get to do that when they are little. Activities in Auckland are expensive — MOTAT, Rainbow's End, the zoo. Here the entertainment is free.

Look at all my animals, for a start: the children who visit just love them. They run around after the animals all the time, even if the animals aren't exactly thrilled about it. In the city, children are so limited in their choice of pets. Here, we can go overboard. There is always a variety of birdlife on the lake, where they're pretty safe from rampaging children. One white swan made its home here last winter, and a pair of black swans, too. There are various ducks, mostly mallards, and we've been given three Swedish Blues that we've named Bjorn, Benny and Agnetha — or ABBA collectively. They hatched six ducklings, but one by one the hawks got them — they're pretty hopeless parents. That's because they insist on dividing their time between swimming on the lake and roaming the horse paddocks, pinching remnants of feed from the horse bins, so the poor ducklings, straggling along behind, are easy pickings for the soaring hawks. Sounds cruel, but hawks have to eat too.

In summer the lake is such a restful picture, with the waterlilies in full bloom — large white flowers against the backdrop of the deep green leaves, and the welcome swallows swooping and dipping, snapping up the midges that gather over the surface of the water. All day you can listen to the waterfowl calling to each other; I never grow tired of that sound.

***

The first of August is officially every horse's birthday — foaling day — though my mares tend to foal a bit later, around September or even into November. However, I could be upstairs sorting out details about painting or plastering with the contractor from Masterton when suddenly I'll get a yell from Simon: 'Horse float's on its way up the drive!' The driver's early — we don't even have the horses in the yard yet. Thank goodness for Jemma Broad, my Man Friday, who came to work as a groom for a week in March 2015 and stayed on through Christmas that year. Tall, willowy, born in New Zealand to British parents, Jemma can turn her hand to anything: bringing snacks out to the veranda when I'm caught up with visitors, looking after the dogs, gardening, helping Simon build houses for the growing poultry population . . .

Horse trucks wait for nobody, so Jemma and I rush out to catch the three horses destined to be loaded onto the huge Majestic horse truck and driven away. First on is a pregnant mare belonging to Sam, which is going back to his place at Little Avondale Stud to have her foal: a short ride for her. Then there's my racehorse, a three-year-old with the stable name of Snuff. She'll be dropped off at Opaki, in Masterton, to her trainer, Gerald Innes, and hopefully we'll soon be celebrating wins and places under my racing colours of black with a green Maltese cross, and buttercup armbands and a buttercup cap. Fingers crossed. Last on is a two-year-old bay going to Gareth Baird in Bulls to be broken in. She's never been floated before, but after she's had a good sniff of the ramp and heard the other horses whinny, Simon and Jemma firmly place their hands on her rump and she willingly walks right on up into the truck. Watching them leave from her paddock is my superstar grey mare Maggie O'Reilly. She recently foaled a filly foal to Sam's sire Per Incanto, and it's a huge relief to have a live foal from her as I can't begin to tell you how much angst she's caused me trying to get her pregnant.

Off down the drive they go, in the safe hands of the driver, who knows, when he's driving with horses on board, to go around every corner as if he has a load of crystal chandeliers in the back. Horses and polo ponies that get carted around to races, shows, hunts and matches do, over time, get used to bracing themselves as the truck or horse float goes around corners, but babies on board for the first time can go down and injure themselves with a cowboy driver.

Now what? If the phone is ringing it could be an enquiry from someone about having a wedding here. They'll need to know pricing details, if there is nearby accommodation, and a multitude of other queries. Most of our enquiries come via email, and I'll direct people to our website. I'll also send them a pricing structure that includes what they can expect in that package. I tell them about accommodation in the area, and give them a small hireage list plus some accessories to the wedding, such as outdoor games like pétanque that they can play. We also offer extras for the bridal party if they want to get ready here before the wedding. They can do all sorts of things — have a claybird shoot, golf, a big lunch. You name it, pretty much, and we'll provide it.

***

Thanks to Simon, my groundsman, we've got a vege garden full of produce. Under his long tunnel house he's raised a huge variety of vegetables from seed: tomatoes, including heirloom ones for Mum, climbing peas and snowpeas, brassicas, purple carrots, chillies, watermelons, and sunflowers again because they were so successful in the past, stretching up higher than any of us, even Jemma, who's over six feet tall.

It takes Simon four, nearly five hours to mow the lawns on the ride-on, and that includes the tennis court, collecting the clippings and emptying them into the compost and doing the edges. I wouldn't like to do it, with the gnarly slopes near the edge of the lake and the rock wall right in the middle of the spreading front lawn. In the past, when we were kids, Mum had a man helping in the garden for 14 years, called Hamish Kummer. One day he got into huge difficulty with our great beast of a mower called the Clinton. It was one of those older types with a roller on the front and a much bigger roller on the back. It looked like a hand-mower, but it was a motor-mower with a clutch, and it went so fast you had to almost run behind it to keep control of it. Dad had actually banned Hamish from using the mower, for his own sake, but once when Dad was away he did use it and it ran out of control, cut straight through all Dad's oak seedlings he'd been raising for years, shot across the lawn and demolished the brick wall. Mum came flying out through the front doors and found a couple of red legs sticking out from the pile of bricks — a pukeko had copped it.

We contemplate what to do with the two pigs, Grunt and Mama. Do we keep them for another breeding season or turn them into sausages and bacon? Grunt is a Large White breed, and Mama is a Saddleback. They both had piglets late last year. Boris the boar was the father; he lives over at the neighbours' place. We either sell the piglets as weaners when they're six or eight weeks old, or raise them here then send them off to a good home-kill place and sell them then. It's quite a good income, and it means we also have our own source of hams for weddings and events. I know that visitors find it weird that we have cute little piglets running around that we care for and feed every day, watching them get fatter on our scraps, only to take them away to be killed and then eaten. My philosophy is, if you're not a vegetarian, then let's give these animals a good life and slaughter them in a humane fashion. I can guarantee that with my pork, whereas I don't know where the meat comes from that you buy at the supermarket, all wrapped in plastic. Grunt and Mama certainly live the good life here at Te Parae. They've had their third litters now, and they will last a lot longer here than if they lived in a commercial piggery.

Over the fence by the front gate when you drive into Te Parae you might see a black Angus steer with horns, along with a couple of horses. The steer is Bounce. Bounce should have been mince, steak, corned beef and brisket by now, but he's still running around the paddock eating grass. He turned up when he was a week old, given to me by one of my cousins, Bec Hardgreaves, because he'd fallen off a trailer and grazed nearly all the skin off his scrawny little body. That's why I called him Bounce — he'd bounced off the trailer. Bec, who is married to the local ranger, took him to the vet and had him patched up and castrated, but it was touch and go whether he'd survive.

Bounce had other ideas. He guzzled down the milk I fed him, enjoyed being looked after and kept on growing. He was meant to be killed for tucker and halved with my cousins, and every now and then I take a photo of him and text it to them and they text back and say, 'Yum.' But I find it a bit hard to turn him into food because, if I go out there and call him, he'll come up to me. He won't let me pat him now, though. Because he wasn't de-horned as a calf he has grown these enormous horns, which is a clear sign to stay well away of him. Also this may give me some distance to cut the apron strings before he'll be killed for the freezer!

I do get emotionally attached to my animals; they are like our children. In fact, they are substitutes for the children we don't have. Everyone says you should never name your stock, the ones that will end up dead before your eyes, but we do. The pigeons have names, the Swedish Blue ducks, all the chooks and the doves. The get their own little pet cemeteries, too: Brian the fawn, Bear the Labrador and Mr Peacock are all buried in Marky's Garden beside the 60-year-old azalea.

Then there's Hector the pet lamb. He was never killed, unlike the pet lambs of other kids whose fathers quietly took their lambs away one day, then lied and said they were out the back of the farm enjoying life with all the other sheep. Our lamb's full name is Hector Rodriguez and he was found motherless, lying in a ditch, nearly dead, and brought back to my kitchen to be revived. For months he thought he was a dog and followed me around the pantry and kitchen, much to the disgust of the two black Labradors and the amusement of any visitors. Now he lives over at Tim's place with Lunch, another pet lamb that has grown huge, and Tim has the task of shearing them. He knows he's never going to end up basted and roasted then carved up and served with gravy, peas and mint sauce — even though Simon can't help but see Hector on his plate!

My dogs keep me company all through the day — not that I get lonely; I'm far too busy. I was way more isolated sitting in my office in Queen Street at Louis Vuitton. By the time I've fed the horses and dogs, made sure the horses are locked up, and returned the escaping piglets to their pen, there's no time for feeling lonely.

Old Hine-Waka might not come out around the paddocks with me any more, but, considering her advanced age, it's fair to say she's earned the right to lie around all day in a warm spot. In the winter she'll stay close to the woodburner in the kitchen, but as soon as the days warm up in the spring and summer she makes her way to the veranda and snoozes in the sun. Despite her age she's happy and pretty mobile; I wouldn't keep her around if she was suffering. Waka's a heading dog, originally from Weber in Hawke's Bay. She was given to Dad by Harvey Beetham, and Guy used her on the farm as his main eye dog. She was fantastic at moving deer around the yards. Heading dogs are prized for their quick movements and superb visual skills when herding sheep. They're descended from Border Collies, and purebreds are black and white like Waka. They're extremely intelligent and love to work. If they're left idle for too long they've been known to herd little kids, ducks and chooks, and they can get themselves into trouble by herding sheep into corners of paddocks and smothering them. The other main type of working dog is the huntaway, which will go to the back of the flock and bark.

Some years ago Waka was hit by a car that was roaring along the big long straight out here. Guy took her to the vet, who said, 'You can either fuse her shoulder or have her put down. The choice is yours.' There was no choice as far as Guy was concerned, and that's why Waka walks around with one stiff front leg. In winter she wears a little cardie that Jemma knitted for her to ward off the arthritis. She came to us from Guy four years ago.

There are no winter woollies needed for the Labradors — they have a nice subcutaneous layer of fat to keep them warm. Boo was a rescue lab. I got her from a pig hunter on the Wairarapa coast who was using her to breed pig dogs. She'd had a few litters — apparently if you cross a Labrador with other breeds, like pitbulls, you'll end up with a good pig dog — but he no longer had any use for her so he was going to have her put down. When I heard this I said I'd take her and rehome her with another family.

Well, that was three years ago, and she's one of our family now. She's the most loyal dog you could ever find. She follows me to and fro wherever I go, all day long. She will wriggle through the tiniest hole in a fence to be with me. If Jemma goes down the paddock and Boo starts to follow then finds I'm not there, she'll come racing back to find me. She's a lovely dog and she gets on really well with two-year-old Mukwa. Often you'll look out the window and see the two of them rolling around the lawn together, playing and having a great old time.

Mukwa means Grizzly Bear in one of the Native American dialects. She's a descendant of Sparkle Bear — that's the emotional side of me showing, for a rare moment, when I named her. I took her out duck shooting last year for the first time, with mixed results. Dad and I went out together, with the result that she has a lot to learn — she was too busy playing around. After we'd shot a couple of ducks and I walked her around the dam from the maimai, she finally figured it out. We'll see what she does this year.

Sometimes the lawn at Te Parae looks like 'the Black Lab Gang', when my friend Liz's black Lab called Kevin Pollock comes to stay, and my brother Tim's dog Max visits us. Max is Mukwa's brother, and we had to give him a severe lesson in how to behave around poultry a few years back, after he decided he was hungry and ate all four of my beautiful chooks. Now, when he comes to play — and he can saunter over from Tim's by himself — he behaves himself and knows I'm in charge. I don't even have to raise my voice, I just say in a conversational tone, 'About time you tootled off home now, Max,' and he'll trot away home.

The most pampered of all, though, is Harry the greyhound — Harry Hall, also known as HRH. When we moved here, Simon said, 'I'm going to get a greyhound.'

'A greyhound!' I said. 'My grandmother would be turning in her grave. It's racehorses at Te Parae and that's it!'

I didn't stop and think about my grandmother's words to her fiancé Alister, all those years back, when he told her no racehorses: 'No racehorses; no Nancy.' This was ironic. Afterwards, when I remembered that Simon was coming to live in our family home while here I was giving him a hard time already, I went back to him and sheepishly told him I'd changed my mind, and yes, we should get a greyhound. We went online and trawled through the Greyhounds as Pets website, looking for a suitable dog for Te Parae. It had to be one that didn't like cats; we don't want cats here, so they need to be chased away. It had to be housetrained too — some of them aren't. Finally we found Harry and he seemed to fit the bill. He'd only won one out of his 20 races and that, according to his owners, was because he was too sociable with the other dogs. So Harry Hall was being retired.

Well, it was like adopting a child. Two people from Greyhounds as Pets came out to inspect us and this place, where Harry Hall would be living. They looked all around Te Parae Homestead: 'Where will Harry sleep?' they enquired.

'Out in a cage like Boo and Mukwa, of course,' I said.

'No, no, that will not do,' they protested. 'Greyhounds have very little fat on them.'

'Where should he sleep then?'

'Inside. He needs a bed.'

The upshot of all this is that now His Royal Highness sleeps on our $4000 sofa with a feather duvet. Every night he slips into his Hugh Hefner-style dressing gown. Jemma has also made him a Batman outfit and he has an outdoors Barbour coat. If the two Labs ever try to get on the couch with him he snarls at them, which is the only time he ever shows any sign of bad temper; Harry is the kindest, friendliest, quietest pet. He once ran away out the gate and down the road and ended up in the pound because nobody in the district believed any farming family would be mad enough to own a greyhound. But we are, and we love him. He is now well known in the district!

***

Of course it's hard work caring for this menagerie. As well as the pets I've already talked about, there are the four Red Shaver chooks making a nuisance of themselves around the stables, Arthur the white dove, and three grey fantail pigeons called Patricia, Paris and Percy. The great thing about having all these pets at Te Parae —

aside from the fact I've always loved animals and am lucky enough to have the space for them to lead a good life here — is that when we have a function on the property the guests are enchanted. The chooks might be terrorised by visitors' children, but, the kids think it is awesome to collect one warm brown egg and be told they can take it home and boil it for their breakfast. Most children today see their eggs come in a cardboard carton; they have no concept of what the term 'free range' really means.

When I was selling luxury handbags and designer-brand products I never thought I would need to learn about pasture management: when to fertilise for optimal growth, what soil type we have, and stock rotation. God, I thought that was why Mum and Dad had three boys — they'd be the ones to deal with that. But I've found that I can rely on support from our local community and that is truly inspirational. You can't beat rural communities for the feel-good factor, and the Wainuioru area is second to none. It also helps having a brother — Tim — who fertilises farms from the air for a living.

In the last five years we've spent much of our time tidying fences, troughs and pastures on our 100-acre block. All my life I've lived with the old ones and thought they looked perfectly acceptable; I just took it all for granted. It wasn't until Kevin the fencer had finished his work that I saw the difference. Everything looked so much better with the posts upright instead of angled every which way, and with the wires straight and taut.

I have had to try to get down with the farming lingo, and that means there are times I will throw in the occasional comment like 'dry-matter ratio'. Now, I have no idea what that means, but it sounds intelligent. Having to communicate with cockies instead of fashion designers, and talk farming — albeit on a very light scale — to (mostly) men who have been in the industry for 40-odd years is in itself a challenge, but that's never stopped me before; it's just another bullet point to add to my now very varied and colourful CV.

The first major purchase Simon and I made after moving back to the Wairarapa was a chainsaw each. We then spent two years cutting unwanted trees from around the lake, trimming oak and maple boughs from the garden, and poisoning elm suckers that would sprout up metres away from the older trees. Once a month we would have a burn pile, sending smoke signals all over the district. Mum and Dad would arrive up the drive and I could see the looks in their eyes as yet another 80-year-old tree hit the deck. Dad's been great with all the requests I've put to him about clearing out some of the trees he planted so I can develop a space for a future permanent marquee. I needn't have worried my head about it in the middle of the night; that was a waste of time. 'Oh yeah, Mouse, go for it,' he said. 'That's a great idea. I only planted those trees because they were there.' And there's a bonus to all these trees meeting their demise: we have an abundance of firewood, which is a relief when open fires are the only source of heating. Central heating in this place? No such thing — just put on another layer of clothing.

Not all trees last forever, and it was with some regret that we decided to take down one or two oaks planted by my great-grandmother. But all is not lost: we have milled the wood into timber, and are looking forward to adding some 90-year-old oak furniture to the homestead interior.

The other major farming-related purchase was a second-hand John Deere tractor. These days, visitors will often find me driving around paddocks harrowing and rolling, trying to bring the pastures back ready for the next onslaught of horses. And for me, this also serves as a bit of time out, thinking time — maybe like those men I've heard about who love to mow lawns or their vineyards, and who use the solitude to think about their businesses.

Things don't always run as smoothly around this place as I

might have suggested. Like the time last year when I escaped for a weekend and let a friend, Alan Griffin (Griffie), loose on his D6 bulldozer and Tim on his 660 chainsaw to fell 'a couple of trees' as part of the next-on-the-list tidy-up area near the stallion boxes, which eventually will become guest accommodation. I returned home to find the two trees gone, sawed up in piles, as well as half of the stallion box roof and wall missing. Both Griffie and Tim turned up to the homestead to sheepishly inform me of the state of play. But there was no point crying over spilt milk. We just had to get on and start working on the upgrades, even though this wasn't in the plan for another three years! Hopefully, if there aren't too many interruptions or mishaps, or misreading of my instructions by men with chainsaws and bulldozers, we may soon have a type of 'glamping' accommodation in the stallion boxes for guests to enjoy that 'at one with nature' experience.

Juxtaposed with the work we do felling trees, repairing fences and renovating the homestead, we run the business of not only weddings, but also hosting groups for lunches, dinners and high teas. A standout was the Ferrari Club, with 50 of their precious cars parked on the lawn; how none of them got stuck I'll never understand, considering the enormous amount of rain we'd had the day before. We also host residents from retirement villages in Masterton, Wellington and Palmerston North who, after a talk about the property, will inevitably mention a connection with Te Parae or their parents or siblings who used to work on the property. I enjoyed the exclusive lunches for a group of guests who arrived in eight helicopters; and, a couple of my favourites, Christmas parties for the Brancepeth and Little Avondale staff, who are such a big part of this place.

But the highlights are definitely the weddings — they are romantic, exciting and light up the place. The wedding season for us runs from November to April, aimed at the best of the summer weather. Simon and I made the decision from the outset that we wouldn't cram the numbers through with two or three functions a week. At Te Parae it's about the bridal group sharing their special day, just as it was for us on our wedding day — taking the time in this huge expanse of garden, enjoying the atmosphere, letting the guests roam around the stables, play with the dogs, explore the surrounding area. People come here for only a few hours, or even a day. If they can, they spend a few days in the Wairarapa, and much of it in or around Te Parae with us. So my generation is making it work by hosting these functions — that's the new commercial legacy for the homestead. We see some incredible weddings held at Te Parae, from the small and intimate to the large and loud. No two couples are the same and neither are the weddings. Lateral thinking is probably one of the best skills to have, as not all weddings run smoothly; the goalposts frequently move.

We haven't had too many guests do outrageous things; people are fairly well behaved. We're more likely to see things from outside the box at our own parties, with family and friends. We've hosted parties with themes like 'What you wore when the ship went down', where guests swam, waterskied and sailed across the lake; and the TV show *The Love Boat*, where we acted out the welcoming committee with Julie the Cruise Director and Captain Stubing rowing our guests across the lake in the *Pacific Princess*. There have also been Bugsy Malone fancy-dress dinner parties where we danced to 'My Name is Tallulah', and a tennis tournament where guests dressed in whites and played with racquets from the 1960s.

Hosting weddings is not all about being glamorous or cruising down easy street. As disorganised as I feel with what I do around Te Parae, I need to be a little of everything, from a counsellor wiping away stress-induced tears, to the shoe shiner and tie straightener, to pinning corsages and being an electrician when the lights short out. My tasks can range from plunging the blocked Portaloo at 11 pm to chasing the preoccupied MC to get the show back on track! It's all hands on deck, and my responsibility is to make sure the couple drive away (or are driven away) having experienced one of the best days ever.

Every wedding is different, from set-up and the bridal party all the way through to the coordination of every little detail on the big day. To give you an example of what gets thrown at you — and this demonstrates the uniqueness of Te Parae as a wedding venue — for one particular wedding, the party also had the groom and his groomsmen getting ready before the ceremony at Te Parae. While I was doing things like taking the groom's party claybird shooting, serving them open fillet-steak burgers with cheese and petit-fours platters, then setting up the ceremony area, I looked up to see a swarm of bees cruising about over the lake. Normally I wouldn't think twice about this, but it did seem a bit odd that they were not moving on. Then things started to go from bad to worse. I was over in the area sorting out the final touches on the ceremony area, draping ribbons and flowers along the walkway, when I looked up to see the swarm settling nicely on the bough of the Wellingtonia tree directly above where the couple were to be wed. This was only a matter of hours before kick off. Great.

Trying to keep calm, I suggested to the groom's party that maybe this would be a good time to start getting changed into their finery for the ceremony. Once the boys were out of the way I raced inside and rang Dad, who is well experienced with bees, having owned many hives over the years. 'Dad, get over here now,' I said. 'We have an emergency. There are bees in the tree above the ceremony area and I have guests arriving in one hour!' He arrived with two nucleus boxes and a whole lot of hope that they would eventually move from the tree into the boxes. I, on the other hand, was having a nervous breakdown. All I could think of was watching the guests swatting bees for the duration of the ceremony; or, even worse, the person who inevitably — and there is always one — has an acute allergy to bee stings and goes into anaphylactic shock.

The only alternative was to move all the chairs and haybales — which the guests sit on like pews — to another spot in the garden. But by now there was only half an hour before the guests were meant to start arriving and this would be just what they wanted to see — me dragging a hundred chairs and bales of hay all over the front lawn! I was starting to feel like the character out of the movie *Four Weddings and a Funeral*, where the slightly goofy brother had to make up an excuse to the bride to buy more time, waiting for the groom to get to the altar because of his second thoughts; his story was to move guests because of the number of people who suffered from hayfever. Here I was trying to assure the groom all was fine, no problem, just a teeny-weeny, slight issue of uninvited guests in the form of a huge swarm of bees — several thousand — directly above their heads when they exchanged vows. Amazingly the groom, groomsmen and minister all seemed to be very relaxed, and thought it was a nice country feel. They were happy for all to remain exactly as it was. I, on the other hand, was thinking of all the worst-case scenarios, and politely said, 'So long as you inform all the guests of the hazard,' — the PC-ness coming out in me — 'and if anyone wants to sue me tell them not to bother because I don't have any money.'

The bride arrived a short time later, very nervous, like most brides, and I made an executive decision there and then not to tell her anything about the bees. 'Don't mention the bees' was the word of the day. It would have been a teensy bit too much for her to take in, at that point in time. So off she went down the aisle, the ceremony took place, and coincidentally, right on cue, the bees did find their way into the hives, with only the odd one buzzing about.

The ceremony went ahead without a hitch, and not even one guest swatting — or suing.

We recently had a bough off the old oak fall onto the marquee lawn. It was in between weddings so luckily no marquees were up, but we did have one going up in a few days. The damage that would have been caused if a wedding was in action — I shudder to think of the consequences! So out came the chainsaws and away we went, again stocking the wood shed for the winter. And then a phone call to the local arborist to come out to check all surrounding trees.

In another case of nature rearing its head before a ceremony, I was out weed-eating around the ceremony area when I disturbed a wasp nest! I threw down the weed-eater, ear muffs and goggles and ran for my life, arms flailing desperately to ward off the wasps! Not one to be beaten by a wasp nest, Simon and I went back that night and threw a couple of teaspoons of carbaryl in the hole . . . no more wasp nest.

***

It's hard graft, and I often ask myself if I'm getting anywhere. I'm always trying to do everything perfectly, correctly. When will I be satisfied? When the bank manager stops hounding me! Seriously, though, I do get a huge kick out of it. And the best positive feedback is what we get from locals — when someone says they have friends who got married at Te Parae and they just loved it, and the old place looked magnificent. That's huge praise for me, and it keeps me going. Or when family members tell me I'm doing a great job: 'Good on you for taking this on.' They appreciate that we're taking this to the next generation.

Angela and Mark.

CHAPTER EIGHTEEN

My Te Parae

What does this homestead
mean to me today, now that
I have said goodbye for ever
to the glamour of city life and
all the Louis Vuitton luxury?
To say it's a magical lifestyle
doesn't do it justice —
the space, the animals, the
beautiful garden in spring
and summer that rewards all
your hard work — all those
are things that are sometimes
easy to take for granted,
even though it's hard work
maintaining them in
good order.

Without hesitation, I would say it is the people who make Te Parae — the homestead, and the community around it — such a special place for me and my family. Everyone, it seems, who comes into contact with this place has their own special memories of times spent here. Some, like Bart Cummings, might remember having the best duck à l'orange ever. Others, like our former nannies, some of whom have married and stayed on in the Wairarapa, recall how welcoming Mum and Dad were.

JoJo and I still catch up from time to time, and she talks about how very young she was when she came to Te Parae, and how trusting Mum was — perhaps too trusting when she let JoJo, who had barely driven a car, take her little sports car to Wellington over the Rimutaka Hill to return 10 pairs of shoes that Mum had brought home on appro from Ashley Ardrey's shoe shop. She also remembers Mum teaching her to always 'cleanse, tone and moisturise', and how to shop!

***

When Marky and I were born, it meant Mum had four children under the age of three. She and Dad used to go away quite a lot for horse business — racing, visiting other horse studs and looking out for new stallions — and because there were always people coming to Te Parae who needed to be formally entertained, she really needed help with us children: she was, in essence, doing two fulltime jobs. She decided to get a nanny — or, as they were in those days, a trained Karitane nurse.

From what I've heard passed down in family stories there were several applicants who took one look at us boisterous kids and fled. But then along came Viv Saywell, an extremely capable 19-year-old, born and bred in the Wairarapa on Swamp Road (now called Matarawa Road). We couldn't have asked for anyone better. Viv, with her ability to cope with whatever emergency was thrown at her, was made for the job.

Viv didn't just look after us four; she looked after Buzz and Susie's children, too — Sam, Anna when she came along, three years after me, and then George a year later. Looking back, I don't know how Viv did it. She's one of those no-nonsense, positive people and she has an enormous sense of humour. She remembers, the first night she was here, everyone crowded into the Te Parae kitchen for a drink to celebrate her arrival — Nat Clarke the stockman, Fred the gardener, plus all the Williams family. She says now that she was so delighted to find there was no snobbery or demarcation between bosses and employees. However, with so many individuals coming and going at the busy homestead it took her some time to work out that Dick, Richard and Buzz weren't three people but one and the same — Uncle Buzz.

Viv is now Viv Fauvel. She married Ralph Fauvel, a farmer, and we still keep in touch. They live just out of Carterton, up the top of a twisty road called The Admiral that has views almost from Featherston to Masterton and across the Tararua Range. She has very accurate memories of bringing us up, and whenever I spend an afternoon with her I leave with aching, tear-stained cheeks from laughing so much.

Timmy was especially mischievous, as Viv puts it. She insists he wasn't naughty: 'cheeky and irrepressible' is the worst she'll say, and 'lippy'. 'He had this white-blond hair with blue eyes, and one day I was in town with him — he was in the pushchair and Guy was walking alongside. You two twins were at home with your mother. I had to get into the ANZ bank, up these steps, and this elderly lady came along. She was all dressed up in a nice coat with a hat, and she had her walking stick, and she was very nicely spoken. She stopped and looked at Timmy and she said, "What a dear little girl you are." And Timmy looked at her and said, "I'm a boy, you stupid bitch!"'

It wasn't as if Mum or Dad spoke like that, but Timmy liked to hang out with the grooms in the stables, or the farmhands, and he copied them all the time. Viv would have been horrified and apologised profusely; she was always teaching us good manners. Guy wasn't like that at all; he was always the little gentleman, the responsible one. He always shook hands and was nice to people. He was mostly a good boy, but he was completely overshadowed by boisterous Tim.

Timmy always wanted to play with Guy and Sam, who were only three weeks apart in age. They would tell him he could be the tiger and hunt them, but then they'd dump him and run off. 'I hate you bathdards!' he'd screech, with his slight lisp, after them. 'Why do I always have to be the nasty tiger? You bathdards!' Viv was always trying to get Tim to do his schoolwork when he started at Wainuioru, but he would refuse. He would wind her up deliberately. She'd say, 'You don't spell *we're* without an apostrophe — it doesn't make sense. If you don't learn to spell you won't get a job when you leave school.'

Tim replied, 'Do you know what a sprocket is?'

Of course Viv didn't know what a sprocket was, but he did, so he said, 'Well, you won't get a job at Jensen and Pollet.'

Jensen and Pollet was a motorbike shop in Cole Street, next to the *Wairarapa Times-Age*, where Timmy would escape to whenever we went to town. He was mad on engines. Once, when Viv took all seven of us to a movie, Tim gave her a terrible fright. When we came out of the movie she counted all the heads and there were only six: no Timmy.

'You children stay here,' she told us and she went off to look in all the bathrooms, but she couldn't find him. Then she ran off to all the garages, including Jensen and Pollet, but still no Tim. She was really worried by this stage because she'd never lost a child before, so she rang Buzz. 'I've lost Tim. What will I tell Tom and Gay?'

Buzz wasn't really fussed. 'I doubt they'll care much.'

'But what if someone's stolen him?'

Buzz replied, 'Don't worry, they won't keep him for long.'

As it turned out, Timmy reckoned he'd looked around and couldn't find us so he started walking home. He was found just past the Te Ore Ore Bridge, which meant he'd walked about six kilometres. A local teacher saw him strolling along, stopped and asked this little seven-year-old what he was doing. When Tim said he was walking to Te Parae, the teacher picked him up and took him there.

Viv paints a vivid picture of idyllic chaos at Te Parae, yet in the midst of this happy maelstrom, everyone was made welcome. There were so many people coming and going, and there were black Labradors, ponies and animals everywhere.

There was a young girl working at Te Parae for a while. She had fallen pregnant, and in those days, before it was acceptable to raise a child as a solo mother, she was sent to the homestead to have her baby away from her family and friends and then give it up for adoption. Mum and Dad took her in; that's what they were like, totally non-judgemental. She went into Masterton hospital and had her baby, a little boy, then came back to Te Parae, where Marky and I were babies, and Marky became her substitute little baby boy. It must have been tough for her.

There was always laughter at home, and men being silly. Viv remembers Mum in the kitchen trying to feed her babies while Dad and Uncle Buzz were shooting mice with air rifles. Mum, unlike many women, didn't go into hysterics; she just growled at them a bit and said teasingly, 'Don't do that in here. The slugs will ricochet and kill my babies.'

How does Viv remember me? 'I hold this memory of you, Bub — you were called Bub in the early days — chair pulled up to the sink beside Gay, with your sleeves pushed up, hair pulled back, helping your mother cook. You liked to help with the baking.'

Viv remained close to our family after she left. She later became godmother to my cousin Anna. This isn't unusual in the Wairarapa; it's such a tight community, and even if people aren't related to each other they soon make connections that will last over several generations.

***

Te Parae was important to young men, workers from the stables or the farm, who went off to fight in the two world wars. In fact it was such a mainstay in their lives that many of them recorded Te Parae as their place of residence. Some of them never returned to this place they called home. It's sad they didn't have close family members they could list — mothers, fathers, brothers or sisters — but at least they felt Te Parae was their family.

Private Ivor Edward Champion was one such man. His photograph was published in the *Auckland Weekly News* after he was killed in action in Caterpillar Valley on the Somme, on 27 September 1916. Champion came to Te Parae from Ruawai, worked as a farmhand, then sailed away — to his death. William John Munro was another: he came from Australia to work at Te Parae. When he joined the Mounted Rifles, 25th Reinforcements, he listed his occupation as 'rabbiter', his date of birth as 'unknown', and his next of kin as 'M.C. Hawkins, friend, Te Parae'.

More men followed in World War II. Buried in a corner of the Florence War Cemetery in Italy is Irishman James Barry, farmhand from Te Parae. His date of birth is unknown. He was a sapper, a private in the New Zealand Provost Corps, and he died while still overseas, in January 1946, probably from injury or illness.

One who did make it back to the Wairarapa to be buried in the

Featherston cemetery is Private Alan Victor Eteveneaux, of the New Zealand Infantry. Again his date of birth is unknown. He is listed as a former farmhand from Te Parae station who, when he signed up, listed his next of kin as 'Mr D. Epplet, Te Parae, friend'.

***

Since returning home I have made a point of catching up with people who worked and lived at Te Parae to listen to their stories. I needed to hear these, because the warmth they say they experienced is exactly what I want to replicate when my guests come here for weddings or events. I want them to feel as welcome as Viv Saywell did on that first night she crowded into Te Parae's kitchen. And I want them to go away feeling a bit like Arthur Ormond felt when he lived at Te Parae as a young man.

Arthur Ormond from Hastings, a leading figure in the thoroughbred-breeding industry today, is someone who credits Te Parae with giving him a good start in his career. He has remained a great friend of our family ever since his first introduction to 'brand Te Parae', as he calls it. He first met Alister in the early 1960s when Alister and his father, Wal Ormond, were both councillors for the Breeders' Association; Alister was later president and Wal was vice-president. Arthur met Alister again in 1967 when he was working for the great Woodville trainer Eric Ropiha; this was his first entry into the world of thoroughbreds. In his time there, Country Girl, an Agricola mare owned by Nancy Williams and leased to Alister and to Joe Saba of Featherston, won four races; and Baloo, raced by Alister's sister Nan Borthwick, won the 1968 Pahiatua Jubilee Cup. Alister and Nancy would often call in to Eric's stables in Gladstone Street when they were passing through Woodville. Arthur says that Eric often talked about his connection to Te Parae, and in particular his training triumph for the family when Ilumquh won the 1960 Caulfield Cup.

Arthur came to live and work at Te Parae in 1968, just after Mum and Dad got married. He still feels bad about invading their privacy. 'Poor Tom and Gay came back from their honeymoon and there I was — up the stairs, first door on the left! Not only did they take me on but they made me feel genuinely welcome: first Buzz and Susie who put me up at their house, Ngaipo, and then Tom and Gay, who looked after me at Te Parae.'

He had been here many times before though, visiting Granny Andy and my grandfather Alister before they moved to Little Avondale, being fed hearty breakfasts in the same kitchen where I now entertain all my workers and casual visitors. Back then, when he started as a junior trainee, his boss was Uncle Buzz. Mark Rimene was stud groom. 'I spent a lot of time working with him,' Arthur remembers. 'Mark and Diane became lifelong friends, and when Mark finished at Te Parae and came to Hawke's Bay we would work together again; as I would with their son, Matthew.'

It's great to hear Arthur speak so highly of how Te Parae influenced him, because he's become such a leading figure in the thoroughbred-breeding industry himself. He was an outstanding president of the New Zealand Thoroughbred Breeders' Association, and he's been made a life member. He reckons he was 'extremely lucky' to be employed at Te Parae when the stud was 'at the top of the tree. Agricola was kicking goals in New Zealand and Australia, and Oncidium was the most exciting stallion prospect in the country.' As well as that, he says, the Te Parae broodmare band, spearheaded by the great Sunbride, was the equal of any in Australasia. Arthur remembers getting to know the road from Masterton to Te Parae very well — to the extent that he could navigate his way back to the homestead after a night on the gin. Uncle Buzz wasn't too happy about that, though. 'I fell into a deep sleep and was woken by pebbles hitting my bedroom window and a running commentary from Buzz underneath, suggesting I get out of bed and get to work.'

Arthur's girlfriend and future wife, Monica, lived over the Rimutaka Hill. Apparently Mum and Dad decided to speed up their courtship by asking Monica over to stay at Te Parae. 'Buzz benefited from this because of the extra help on the foaling lookout, and I was so much more alert!' When the mares are foaling, someone has to be awake in the foaling tower all night, usually on shift from seven pm until midnight, then from midnight until dawn. If a mare starts to foal they either foal her or call for help.

As with everyone I've talked to who lived and worked at Te Parae, there were always stand-out fun times. A highlight for Arthur was when Dad trusted him to take his Tiger Moth up for a spin.

What I love about these stories is that no matter what brought individuals to Te Parae in the first place — whether they were nannies, grooms, stablehands or clients wanting to buy yearlings, or whether they arrived at the homestead as employees or customers — they went away as friends. I want Te Parae to continue weaving that magic.

Te Parae homestead and surrounding grounds, 1985.

Angela with Maggie O'Reilly.

CHAPTER NINETEEN

The next generation

According to Williams family history, Te Parae means 'a clearing in the bush'; it is what my ancestors named this property when they made a place to farm from bush-covered hills and plains all those years ago.

These days there is more pasture than bush, fenced and efficiently farmed with sheep, cattle, a few horses and crops. This is what visitors see from the car window as they near the homestead. Whether you approach Te Parae from Masterton and drive over Limeworks Hill, or come out of Carterton through Gladstone over Kurau Hill, you still have to climb up and over high peaks before dropping down, then swinging into Te Parae Road, turning in through our gates and up the oak-lined drive. It's a pleasant journey — not too many sharp bends, and tarsealed all the way.

Once you turn up our driveway, on any day of the year there'll most likely be horses grazing in the paddocks on either side of the 10-wire fences. They might look up and give you a curious stare or, if it's early in the year and they're young weanlings and feeling frisky, they could pretend to be startled and gallop off on their long, gangly legs, showing the speed they've been bred for.

This is rolling land — hills more than plains. Henry Williams defined 'parae' in his *Dictionary of Maori Language* as 'undulating open country'. When you look at this district now, in the twenty-first century — green pastures in spring and winter, burned brown by sun in summer, divided by neat fencing; shelterbelts carefully planted for stock; tracks across the farms for quadbikes; and comfortable houses with tidy gardens set back from the road — it's hard to imagine what kind of struggle the pioneers went through to turn it from wild, uninhabitable backblocks to productive farmland. But struggle is what my family did — the people who came before me. By hand they hacked through the bush and hauled away huge logs with bullock teams and horses. Using pitsaws, they made timber from some of those native logs and built the homesteads we now live in. They got out of their beds before sunrise, made fences to contain their stock, tried to combat the pests that devastated their new pastures, traded their wool and stock, saved, sweated and sometimes failed.

Simon and I are the fourth Williams generation to live at Te Parae Homestead, and we're determined to leave it in good shape for the fifth generation. I don't know when that will be. I don't have a crystal ball; but there's a lot more work to be done before I hand over the keys and drive out the gate for the last time. Hopefully I'll go out in a box.

I count myself as one of the lucky ones. My great-great-grandfather Thomas Coldham Williams knew the meaning of austerity and had a good head for business. He was the one who put the money into Te Parae after the Beetham family leased the initial block of land and started to feel the financial pinch. Although TC never lived here permanently, when I'm cleaning out cupboards or the stables and I find antique ceramic chamberpots or the old pitsaws, I'm reminded of how tough those pioneers had it back in the nineteenth century: there were no flush toilets or modern plumbing; no chainsaws to clear overgrown poplars beside the big lake in one day, as Simon and I have done.

It's hard slog for us too, no doubt about it, even though we've been here five years now. Mum and Dad are getting on and they can't do as much physical stuff as they once did to help reduce costs — cutting down trees, doing the gardens, prepping the house before the builders or painters arrive to work on renovations. Now it's Simon and me who are stripping paint, sanding, ripping out plumbing, chucking old timber out of upstairs windows and hoping the dogs aren't in the line of fire below.

Back in great-grandfather's day this place had so many staff it was definitely not my great-grandmother messing around with this 'men's stuff'. There were three or four gardeners for a start; people who worked for food and lodging — like the WWOOFers or HelpX workers of today.

Occasionally I get a bit down in the dumps because of the sheer amount of unrelenting physical hard work. Sit down and enjoy a break? Good luck with that. Lunch is usually eaten on the run, and in the weekend, when we think it might be quiet and we can catch up on some time together, we'll no sooner pour a cup of tea than we'll hear the sound of car tyres crunching on gravel. Round the corner of the house will appear friends from town: 'It was such a nice day we thought we'd drive out to Te Parae and pay a visit.' If I'm busy in the middle of doing something I must admit I groan inwardly a little, but then seeing friendly faces, opening a bottle of wine if it's late afternoon, chatting amiably together and hearing their praise about the progress we've made since their last visit always perks me up, so I'm grateful for the impromptu house calls.

It's easy to see why this place is so inviting when I'm out on the veranda in the afternoon sun on one of the old wicker chairs, dogs lolling about on the grass or hiding in the shade somewhere. Wherever you sit there's a view out over the lake and, even if there's a good breeze blowing, the century-old trees keep it sheltered. It's so quiet, too — just the sound of a tui calling, the occasional duck, or a horse whinnying in the paddock behind the trees. I've replanted heaps of lavender to bring the bees, and from spring to summer the numerous wattles cast their pollen in great drifts across the view like big yellow clouds.

***

Then there are the horses; they keep me optimistic. Every September my mares will begin foaling and I'll take them to Little Avondale to deliver their babies. If they're going to be served by the stallion again they'll stay there for about eight to twelve weeks; otherwise they'll come straight back here after about three or four days. Agistment is expensive, and there are no family rates around here.

Last season I had three mares foaling. First was my old grey mare Maggie O'Reilly, which I purchased at the broodmare sale in May 2009 at Karaka. I couldn't get to the sale, so I asked Sam to look at three mares I had circled in the catalogue, and he suggested I go with Maggie O'Reilly. I told him the maximum I wanted to spend and waited nervously by the phone until the call came through: 'Mouse, you got her, but I went over your budget!' That's the last time I'll ask Sam to buy me a horse.

Maggie O'Reilly has produced two foals since then: one I sold as a weanling, and the other was a filly that I have kept and is about to start her racing career. Last season's foal was to Per Incanto. My second foaling mare was Tick Tock Time, a lovely-looking mare by

Savabeel. She's had two foals that will be starting racing careers in 2016, and she also foaled to Per Incanto last season. My last mare, which also had a foal by Per Incanto, is Lutine Belle, a mare by O'Reilly. Like Tick Tock Time, she has had two foals and the elder one is just starting his racing career. I have a couple of other mares, too — WaitAMinute by Centaine, and Zalass by Zabeel. Both are coming into their twilight years, both were visited by Per Incanto last year, and both will see their days out at Te Parae. My small band of broodmares may not be the quality to make the granite memorial stones, but you never know.

It pays to listen to advice from the wise heads in the industry. For a start, their advice is free, and also they have managed to survive in the game, make a living out of it and are still here to tell their yarns. It's not an industry that can be easily navigated and it's not for the faint-hearted; the fly-by-nighters are found out early on. I liken the industry to the Holy Grail of races, the Melbourne Cup: it's all about strategy, resilience and playing the long game.

I'll never walk away from breeding horses. It's something I grew up with, worked in, walked away from and then returned to. It's in my blood, and it will always be a part of my life in some shape or form. Hopefully, when I move on from here, whoever it is in the Williams family who takes over also has a love and passion for horses, working with them, and seeing them grow up then go off to the Karaka sales.

But, apart from the breeding side, on a really good day, and when I have the time, there's nothing I love more than purging my mind of all my business commitments — wedding events and bloodstock matters — by walking out to the paddock to catch my 16-year-old ex-racehorse Jerry, and going for a quiet hack around the farm to enjoy the scenery, the same way as I did after school when I was a kid.

***

There never seems to be an orderly pattern to my day. I might have planned a morning of baking cakes, pies and biscuits to fill the freezer, then cousin Sam will interrupt my routine by phoning to say a trainer wants to see a two-year-old gelding I have in the paddock, so I'll drop everything, go out and get the horses into the stables, give them a quick spruce-up to get rid of the excess mud, then put another visitor on hold while the trainer watches me lead the horse around the yard. We'll lift the horse's feet, discuss his legs — his conformation, shoulder strength, girth shape — and try to gauge what he will mature into.

When the summer wedding season is over, a typical day in winter will involve loading up the quadbike with a couple of bales of hay and half a dozen sacks of individually mixed hard feed (horse nuts), driving out down the slushy, muddy tracks to various paddocks and filling large feedbins with tasty extras for my own mares and any other young horses I'm bringing on for other owners. The horses all have different personalities. Some of the mares are quiet and content to wait for the food to be poured into the container, while others lay their ears back and bare their teeth at any competitor. I caution visitors to keep well clear of their hind legs; nobody wants to be kicked by a horse. The young horses are the same — fussing and kidding around, pushing in where they're not wanted. You have to always remember they're maturing into young stallions. In fact, humans should respect horses at all times. They are, after all, hundreds of kilograms heavier than us, and when they're in groups together in paddocks we should never take them for granted.

But mostly they're just big babies, and I love them. Sometimes I think owning horses is a dangerous addiction — it's expensive, time-consuming and you can never seem to give it up, even when you're old and past riding. But, when it comes to thoroughbreds, it's a particularly expensive addiction. Like all addictive pursuits, it has its ups and its downs. The highs are the tremendous pleasure and satisfaction you get from being around horses — grooming them and working with them. I suppose it's similar to the feeling other people get from doing yoga or other relaxing workouts.

If you asked me the deep question of why I really like working with horses, I'd say it's something I know well, having being brought up with horses from early childhood. I don't feel there is a simple answer. There are lots of different facets to my enjoyment of working with horses. It's all very familiar to me. The joys and challenges thrown up by the industry and by the horses themselves: accidents and illness; horses that don't measure up in terms of being good racers; the enjoyment of seeing your decisions in breeding come to fruition, and dealing with the disappointment when they don't; and the satisfaction of teaching young horses.

I don't break in horses; I breed them to sell between the ages of six and twelve months old — best-case scenario! The odd horse sometimes won't sell in that timeframe; they might be too small for their age, or the horse might have injured itself — not seriously, but the client might want to get a vet check, which takes time, and if that doesn't come out well for the horse then the prospective buyer won't go ahead, or might want to wait and have another vet check done later. Then again, the horse's breed might not be 'fashionable' at the time — that's simply the luck of the draw. If one or all or several of these setbacks occur I keep the horse until it's ready for sale at a later stage.

All my mares will foal at a stud, and for the past 10 years this has been at Little Avondale or Waikato Stud, as these big studs have 24-hour care and all the experience and facilities on hand. The mares and foals then return to Te Parae and settle into the surrounds, and it's there that I provide the initial stages of their education. The foals will begin to be hard fed, and become used to human contact. I like to start teaching the foals to have halters on, to be led and have their feet picked up when they're still nursing. It helps to keep them calm. When they're about five months old — once the foals are weaned — they are given more training: leading around, grooming and having rugs put on them. The more handling horses get at a young age the better they are to deal with throughout their careers, whether it be in a racing stable, in eventing or in the breeding paddock. I'm here to help these little babies accept a halter, a rope; it's all about human contact. Some of them are very hot-headed and highly strung; sometimes they have a bad day and a meltdown and there's nothing you can do about it. You can't fight them; you just have to walk away, leave them to settle and try again. They can't be allowed to get away with it, though — maybe like naughty children! But I always remember we're dealing with an animal that weighs in the vicinity of 200 kilograms as a weanling, and will grow to be as heavy as 500 kilograms.

Yes, there have been disasters, though not too many. I like to think that's because of my methods, which are mostly gentle and patient; I don't force a horse to do anything it's not ready to do. After we got Harry the retired greyhound, I took him out with me to the horses. He'd never been out in the open country before, and when he spotted a horse across the paddock he took off like he'd been shot up the backside. I have never seen a greyhound run so fast in real life — by golly, they can go! The horse spotted this black streak coming towards her and bolted straight for the 10-wire fence. I thought, Oh my God, I can't watch this. I covered my eyes, because I was at the top of the hill, by the stables, and couldn't do a thing to stop this train wreck — or horse wreck, to be precise — from unfolding before my eyes. The horse leapt the fence into the macrocarpa shelter plantation, crashed through the trees then jumped the second 10-wire fence out the other side. In the process she stripped the skin off her shins and was standing there with the bones exposed and the skin hanging off, and her cover ripped to shreds. What a mess. Mouse, how could you be so stupid, I thought to myself. I called the vet out to have a look and to try to fix it up.

'All I can do, Angela,' he said, 'is cut that skin away and then we'll bandage it all up and hope for the best.' The horse ended up with just a couple of small scars to show for it. Her siblings and family are starting to show a bit of promise on the track, so maybe she could begin her broodmare career.

I guess Harry didn't mean to mistake a horse for a rabbit. All I will say — in print — is that he was chastised and now is a thorough gentleman around horses.

Disasters — or near-disasters, like that one — are to be expected on farms, and although it happened not long after we had returned home it certainly didn't make me regret coming back. For one thing, if we changed our minds we'd have to rehome Harry and the other three dogs. We couldn't squeeze them into a two-bedroom apartment with a balcony in Grey Lynn, and anyway I'm sure they'd be utterly miserable trying to cope with city life, being taken for walkies in Victoria Park on a leash.

I wouldn't trade this lifestyle for anything now, despite the occasional times I wake in the night tossing and turning with anxiety — and those moments are increasingly less frequent. I'd never go back to the city, even if you tried to tempt me with fancy handbags and glitzy restaurant openings. Simon sometimes says he misses the team environment he loved when he was investigating serious crimes out in South Auckland. In his work down here as a racing investigator he's pretty much on his own; he doesn't have the camaraderie of other like-minded investigators. On the other hand, he felt we'd started to outgrow our social life in Auckland — the Ponsonby Road bars and nightclubs scene — so the offer to buy Te Parae came at the right time.

Our future lies firmly at Te Parae, no matter what obstacles we face. We know there is more back-breaking work to be done, but we're in this for the long haul. I look out of the window and see Griffie on his bulldozer and tractors — the same ones he used for Dad — cutting all these trees down for us, helping us at no cost because he loves seeing what we're doing: preserving this place and taking it through to future generations. That's what keeps me going.

Or the likes of Doon and Sandra Finlayson, friends from Masterton, who come out during their days off to help us with splitting wood, patching up holes in the roofs around our buildings . . . it kind of helps that Doon is a roofer! Sandra has helped out with many functions and weddings, because they support what we are trying to do here and want to be a part of the next stage of Te Parae.

My cousin Bec Hardgreaves has also been an enormous support to us, a chef by trade who will inevitably be given the SOS call to come out and help cater for 45 guests and get paid in firewood. Or Bec's Mum, Aunty Joy, who I now consider to be my resident florist. She will come out and produce beautiful floral displays throughout the homestead for all my functions and weddings, and at no charge!

Of course we'd dearly love a money tree growing out the back. The old place does require a little spruce up here and there. You initially think this would be reasonably straightforward — a lick of paint and a spot of new wallpaper to freshen it up, but that's not how it works with a historic homestead. As they say, we opened up a can of worms. Not only do I have a reputation to uphold, with Mum's exquisite renovation and furnishing of 12 rooms that has lasted 40 years, but I need to try to keep the new renovations in line with the age of the house, all while keeping the budget from blowing apart.

When so many rural homesteads these days are being carved off from sheep-and-cattle stations and sold out of family ownership, I'm determined to hold on to what we have here and keep it in the family. If an overseas investor came along tomorrow and offered us moonbeams, or if we won Lotto, I'd never be tempted to sell up and leave. What would we do? Where would we go for a better life than this one? This is just the start of our journey here. We have four bedrooms to spruce up, and the large hallway and two bathrooms — and that's just upstairs. Luckily we have a few years ahead of us to spread the load.

Along the way we'll continue to breed thoroughbreds on a small scale, and have a couple of shares in the racing stock we've bred. We're also enjoying watching our latest acquisition speeding around the tracks — a racing greyhound, which will no doubt end up at Te Parae to enjoy his retirement. I wonder what Harry will think of that, if a new greyhound tries to join him on the couch and snuggle under the feather duvet.

I am very passionate about preserving this historic homestead from decay and destruction. I'm also concerned that it doesn't move out of the Williams family. At the same time, we want to share this lifestyle beyond the family. It's a labour of love, yes, but it's also a business, and a gratifying one at that. We are getting to the stage where weddings are booked up two years in advance, and I'm getting quite a number of PR companies in Auckland wanting to do corporate retreats down here for weekends — they email or ring us out of the blue and ask for details to be sent. That's massive, for me; I feel we've turned a corner.

Te Parae will always be a place for people from all walks of life to enjoy, whether they're working, visiting, partying or exchanging wedding vows. It has been like this from the beginning and we won't meddle with tradition. It's a struggle but in the end, for Simon and me, it comes down to what really matters: welcoming people into our historic country homestead to share the idyllic family happiness of the place where I was raised.

When I look back at the characters in my history, beginning with Henry and Marianne Williams, down through my pioneering family to Mum and Dad, who have been such an amazing support to me throughout, it hasn't been such a difficult decision after all. My journey through all those years has been worthwhile. It has at times been heartbreaking — especially coping with the loss of my twin brother, Mark — and other times exhausting — such as chasing up ridiculous bureaucracy for luxury handbags held up by Customs. Yet all those experiences have come together to prepare me for this: a life I love and a life with purpose, to keep the 110-year-old Te Parae Homestead alive, happy, welcoming people, and facing a strong future into the next century.

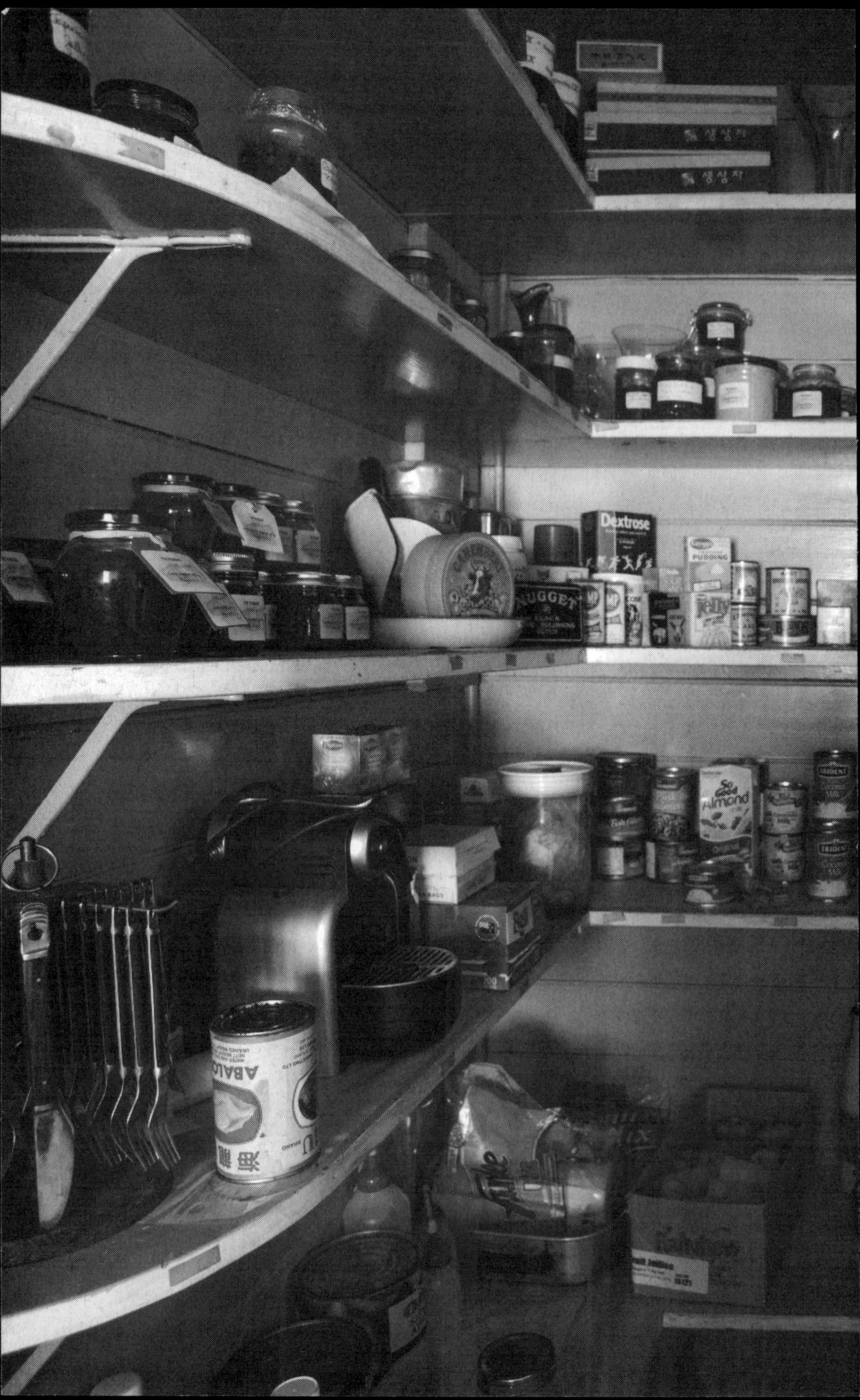
Dextrose
PUDDING
NUGGET
So Good
Almond

Te Paşae recipes

These are some of the recipes I use for small functions, parties or last-minute lunches to share with family and friends. Some are from Mum, others from my travels through Europe and New Zealand. They're great to have in the recipe pile, but it won't take you long before you can do them blindfolded.

When I was young I would often see Mum busily copying a recipe from a magazine in the dentist's and doctor's waiting rooms, sometimes from television, or asking to keep restaurant menus. I would think, Why are you doing that? It seems such a waste of time. Scarily, I now catch myself doing the same thing — though I use a cellphone to take photos rather than hand-write!

Mum bought each of us our first recipe folder to collect recipes when we were 10 years old. Of course at the time I thought it wasn't the most exciting present, but I thank Mum now, 30 years on whenever I look at my poor little bulging folder, chock-full of recipes from all corners of the world. Then I look at Mum's recipe folder, which should almost have its own postcode it's so large! Only she can find things in it . . . a maze of culinary delights for all occasions and generations.

Since I have come home to live at Te Parae, I have started to pickle, bottle, bake and freeze produce each season. From japonica apples to quinces, crab apples to lemons, wild mushrooms to elderflowers — if it's there, I will have a go at turning it into something edible. Poor Simon, I see his eyes roll back when he walks into the kitchen and I corner him to be my taste tester!

Duck à l'orange

Trying to find recipes in Mum's filing system is like nailing jelly to a wall, so after nagging her to find the duck recipe that so charmed Bart Cummings, this was her response: 'I can't find the original recipe but from memory, here goes.'

Stuffing
1 medium onion, roughly chopped
½ orange, peeled and chopped (reserve other half for roasting)
2 sticks celery, chopped
2 slices white bread, ripped up
approximately 2 tbsp melted butter

Duck
1 wild duck or store-bought duck
50g butter, melted
salt and pepper to taste
2–3 rashers streaky bacon
½ orange
3 sticks celery
½ cup beef stock
1 tbsp brandy

First, shoot your duck. Second, make your husband pluck it.

Preheat the oven to 180°C.

Make the stuffing by mixing together all of the ingredients except the butter. Stir in the butter a little at a time, until the stuffing is not dry but not too wet.

Brush duck with butter and sprinkle with salt and pepper. Stuff the cavity of the duck with prepared stuffing.

Cover breasts with bacon and then cover the duck with grease-proof paper.

Place the duck in a roasting pan on top of the orange half and celery sticks. Pour in beef stock.

Cook for approximately 1½ hours. Remove the grease-proof paper halfway through cooking.

Continued overleaf . . .

Orange sauce
- 3 tbsp flour
- 2 tbsp lemon juice
- 2 cups store-bought orange juice
- 1 cup beef stock
- ¼ cup port
- 2 tbsp red currant jelly or crab apple jelly

Garnish
- 1 orange, peeled and sliced
- 1 tsp marmalade (optional)

When cooked, remove from the oven and place on a clean oven tray, reserving the cooking juices in the roasting pan. Pour brandy over the duck. Cover with tin foil and let rest while you make the sauce.

Place the pan that the duck was cooked in on a medium–low heat, add flour and stir with a wooden spoon until bubbling (approximately 2–3 minutes). Add lemon and orange juices, stirring all the time, then add beef stock. Keep stirring the sauce until all the cooked bits left from the duck have lifted from the pan, then bring to boil and simmer for 4–5 minutes. If it looks a little thick add more stock. Add port and jelly. Cook for a further 10 minutes.

Carve the duck, pour over the orange sauce and decorate with orange slices, fresh or fried quickly in a hot buttered pan with marmalade.

Chicken Salad

This is an oldie but a goodie that came from the Melrose Place girls during my time in Auckland. Mum has shared this with many people, and it was included in Wanganui Collegiate's fundraising cookbook. It was one of several recipes we contributed, because Mum was the mother of four former pupils.

Dressing
¾ cup mayonnaise (store-bought or home-made)
¼ cup sour cream
2 tsp curry powder
2 tbsp chopped spring onion
handful of chopped parsley
salt and pepper, to taste

Salad
1 cooked chicken
¾ cup dressing (see recipe above)
2 large lettuces
400g can lychees
3 fresh mandarins, peeled, or 400g can mandarin segments
1 cup chopped celery
1 cup chopped green pepper
handful of chopped parsley, to garnish

To make the dressing, mix all ingredients in a food processor.

Remove chicken meat from bones and toss in ¾ cup of dressing; reserve the rest. Arrange lettuce leaves in a large salad bowl, then arrange layers of chicken, lychees, mandarins, celery, green pepper and dressing over the lettuce leaves until everything is used up. Sprinkle chopped parsley over.

Chicken Marbella

Mum got this recipe from her school friend Sue Gordon (née Wall). Remember to prepare this dish the day before and marinate overnight. This recipe makes enough for approximately a dozen people. You can also use drumsticks or chicken pieces.

4 whole chickens, quartered, or 1kg bag frozen chicken pieces, thawed in fridge
1 head garlic, separated, peeled and finely chopped
¼ cup dried oregano
coarse salt and freshly ground black pepper, to taste
½ cup red wine vinegar
½ cup olive oil
1 cup pitted prunes
½ cup pitted Spanish green olives
1½ cups capers with a little liquid from jar
6 bay leaves
1 cup brown sugar
1 cup white wine
¼ cup finely chopped Italian parsley

In a large bowl, combine the chicken pieces, garlic, oregano, salt, pepper, vinegar, olive oil, prunes, olives, capers and liquid, and bay leaves. Cover and leave to marinate, refrigerated, overnight.

Preheat the oven to 180°C.

Arrange the chicken in a single layer in one or two large, shallow baking pans and spoon all the marinade over evenly. Sprinkle chicken pieces with the brown sugar and pour white wine around them.

Bake for 50–60 minutes, basting frequently with pan juices. The chicken is done when thigh pieces, pricked with a fork at their thickest part, have a clear juice (not pink).

With a slotted spoon, transfer the chicken, prunes, olives and capers to a serving platter. Moisten with a few spoonfuls of pan juices and sprinkle generously with parsley.

To serve Chicken Marbella cold, cool to room temperature in the cooking juices before transferring to a serving platter. If the chicken has been covered and refrigerated, allow it to return to room temperature before serving, then reserve some of the juice and spoon it over the chicken before serving.

Deer Liver Pâté

Mum has worked on this recipe over the years, when she and Dad were selling Cervena around the world. She's adapted it and added ingredients, until it is more suited to the flavour of New Zealand deer. First catch your deer. If not, make friends with someone who goes deerstalking and make sure when they tramp out from the bush with their deer carcass they bring the liver with them.

Béchamel sauce
300ml milk
1 thick slice of peeled onion
1–2 blades of mace (or use ¼ tsp freshly grated nutmeg)
3–4 whole black peppercorns
1 bay leaf
50g butter
20g flour
salt and pepper, to taste

Pâté
340g deer liver (about half a deer liver)
110g fatty bacon
5 anchovy fillets

Make the béchamel sauce first. Warm the milk in a saucepan, without letting it boil. Infuse the onion, spices and bay leaf in the warmed milk until it is well flavoured, around 15–20 minutes. Strain, reserving the milk.

Make a roux by melting the butter over medium heat then adding the flour and stirring constantly for 3–5 minutes, until it forms a smooth paste. Don't let it catch. Add the strained milk slowly and, using a wooden spoon or a whisk, stir over a moderate heat until boiling, to make a smooth, thick white sauce. Season well. Pour into a bowl and leave to cool.

1 clove garlic
good pinch salt
3–4 thin rashers streaky bacon (for lining tin)

Next, make the pâté. If you have a mincer, mince the liver and fatty bacon twice; otherwise, chop the liver and bacon up then process in the food processor, using a sharp blade. Pound the anchovies, garlic and salt together in a bowl with a pestle or a heavy wooden spoon. Add to the liver with the cooled béchamel sauce. Beat well.

Line a terrine dish or loaf tin with baking paper, then with streaky bacon rashers. Fill with the liver mixture and set in a larger pan of hot water to halfway up the side of the terrine dish. Cover with buttered paper or baking paper and bake in a slow oven (120°C) for 40–50 minutes. Press lightly with clean weights (or something heavy wrapped in cling film), and leave to cool.

Serve with hot toast.

Korean Bulgogi

This is a great recipe for venison, done on the hotplate of the barbecue or in a heavy skillet on the stovetop. You'll see the recipe calls for sesame salt. When Mum and Dad were given this recipe, the accompanying 'warning' came with it for making sesame salt: 'Heat a large pan, spread the sesame seeds on it when it is hot. DO NOT plan to do anything else while they are cooking — they know when your attention is elsewhere and will burn immediately. Stir constantly while they brown and pop. When they are an even, dark golden brown colour, pulverise them in a food processor or with a mortar and pestle and add approximately 1 teaspoon of salt to 1 cup of seeds.'

450g shoulder or neck venison (sinews removed)

Marinade
2 tbsp soy sauce (tamari is best)
1 tbsp sugar
1 tbsp sesame oil
1 tbsp sesame salt
4 spring onions, chopped in 2–3cm pieces
3 cloves garlic, finely chopped
1 tsp finely chopped ginger
2 tbsp white wine
pinch black pepper

Cut the venison into thin slices across the grain. This is more easily done if the meat is half-frozen.

Marinate in the remaining ingredients for at least 2 hours.

Grill on a hot barbecue plate or in a frying pan for a few seconds each side.

Serve with steamed rice and stir-fried vegetables.

Slow-roast Lamb

Simon and Dad wouldn't forgive me if I didn't include a lamb recipe.

2 heads of garlic (one separated into cloves and peeled)
1 medium leg or shoulder of lamb
6 anchovy fillets
1 bunch celery
1 lemon, sliced thickly
olive oil, to drizzle
salt and pepper
½ cup water
330ml bottle of beer

Preheat the oven to 200°C.

Separate one head of garlic into cloves and remove the skins.

Make small incisions in the lamb meat and fat, and place garlic cloves and anchovies in each of the incisions.

Slice the second head of garlic in half horizontally. Place the two halves of garlic, whole stems of celery and thick slices of lemon in a roasting pan. Place the leg of lamb on top. Drizzle with oil, add salt and pepper, then add water.

Roast in the oven for 60 minutes.

Remove from the oven and pour in the beer. Reduce the temperature to 150°C and roast for another 60 minutes. The meat should pull away from the bone. Squeeze the garlic from the pan into the juices, then drizzle the juices from the pan over the meat.

The Impossible Quiche

Most country people have a variation on this recipe. It's a great standby, and you can whip it up when visitors arrive unexpectedly.

1¼ cups milk
3 eggs
½ cup self-raising flour
50g melted butter
salt and pepper, to taste
1 cup sliced mushrooms or courgettes
1 cup grated cheese

Preheat the oven to 175°C.

Put all the ingredients except the mushrooms or courgettes and cheese in a bowl and mix well. Pour the mixture into a buttered quiche dish. Poke the mushrooms or courgettes down into the mixture, then sprinkle with cheese. Bake for 45 minutes.

Cheese, Bacon and Egg Puff

This lunch dish is another good standby that has been passed down in our family — but it must be prepared the day before. It is good for using up stale bread.

buttered slices of wholemeal bread (enough to line a pie dish)
4 eggs
1 cup milk
1 small tsp mustard
freshly ground black pepper
1 tsp Worcestershire sauce
1 tbsp mayonnaise
½ tsp dried mixed herbs
1¼ cups grated cheese
4 rashers bacon, chopped
2 spring onions, chopped

Line a pie dish with the buttered slices of bread.

Beat together the eggs, milk, mustard, pepper, Worcestershire sauce, mayonnaise and herbs. Stir in the cheese, bacon and onions. Pour into the bread case.

Cover and refrigerate overnight.

Bake uncovered the next day in an oven preheated to 180°C for 45–50 minutes.

Georgie Falloon's Summer Fennel and Rocket Salad

My Wairarapa friend Georgie Falloon gave me this recipe recently. Georgie started Willow Shoes — shoes for women with long feet — and the success of this business is a tribute to her entrepreneurism. Plus she's a great cook.

1 fennel bulb
juice of 1 large lemon
1 tsp brown sugar
several handfuls of fresh rocket

Olive oil dressing
good-quality olive oil
salt and pepper
2–3 cloves garlic, chopped
½ cup grated Parmesan

Slice or chop the fennel bulb into small pieces.

Mix together the lemon juice and brown sugar to a syrupy consistency and pour over the fennel. Let stand for a minimum of 15 minutes, and no longer than 2 hours. Reserve some of the marinade.

Meanwhile, mix together the olive oil, salt and pepper, chopped garlic and grated Parmesan.

Mix the rocket with the fennel. Pour the dressing over, add a little of the marinade juices and combine well.

Savoury Muffins

These are very easy to make — you just mix everything together. They have a strong flavour so I use mini-muffin trays rather than large muffin pans. Be sure to use non-stick trays as it's quite a wet, sticky mixture. The muffins look ugly when they're done, but, believe me, they taste great. If you find the mixture is too sloppy, you can add an extra tablespoon of flour, but err on the wet side. For vegetarians, leave out the bacon.

¼ cup chopped, precooked bacon
1 cup grated cheese
1 packet Maggi onion soup mix
½ cup flour
1 tsp baking powder
250g sour cream

Preheat the oven to 180°C.

Mix all the ingredients together, being careful not to over-mix. Bake for 20 minutes, until a skewer poked into the centre of a muffin comes out clean.

What could be simpler than that?

Salmon Tart

The cream cheese in this tart guarantees it remains moist and juicy — and there'll be no leftovers!

1 quantity of rich shortcrust pastry (see recipe on page 239)
2 big handfuls of fresh baby spinach leaves— enough to cover the pastry base
250–300g smoked salmon (I use salmon pieces)
150g cream cheese, at room temperature
1–2 tbsp capers
5 eggs
1 cup cream (or use ½ cup cream and ½ cup milk)
100g Parmesan, grated
juice of 1 lemon

Preheat the oven to 180°C.

Roll out the pastry to fit a 26cm tart tin. Add baking beans or pie weights and bake the pastry blind for 10 minutes. Remove the weights and bake the pastry for another 5 minutes, then remove from oven.

In the pastry case place the spinach, then the salmon, and top with teaspoonfuls of cream cheese. Sprinkle the capers over, then mix together the the egg and cream and pour over. Add a light sprinkle of Parmesan.

Bake for 15–20 minutes until the tart is golden on top, and there is no movement when you shake the tin gently. Remove from the oven and leave to cool for 10 minutes. Sprinkle with lemon juice before serving.

Rich Shortcrust Pastry

I came across this classic pastry recipe while I was at Leiths cooking school. I still use many recipes and lessons that I picked up from my time there, and not a week goes by when I don't make this pastry.

Makes enough for a 26cm tart.

170g plain flour
pinch salt
100g butter
1 egg yolk
30ml (2 tbsp) very cold water

Sift the flour and salt together. Rub in the butter until the mixture looks like breadcrumbs.

Mix the yolk with the chilled water and add to the mixture. Mix to a firm dough, first with a knife, and then with one hand. It may be necessary to add more water, but the pastry should not be too damp. Crumbly pastry is more difficult to handle, but it produces a shorter, lighter result.

Chill the pastry, wrapped, for 30 minutes before using; or allow it to relax for 30 minutes after rolling out before baking.

Note: to make sweet rich shortcrust pastry for the lemon tart on page 244, mix in 1 tablespoon of caster sugar after the butter has been rubbed into the flour.

Upside-down Spiced Pear Cake

This is a lovely dessert cake, to be eaten with a fork. When we had large cards printed for Te Parae to advertise it as a wedding venue, I printed recipes on the back. This cake features on some of them.

55g butter
100g brown sugar
400g can pears (or use your own preserved pears)
110g flour
½ tsp baking soda
¼ tsp salt
1 tsp ground ginger
2 tsp ground cinnamon
¼ tsp ground nutmeg
pinch of ground cloves
110g brown sugar
150ml milk
55g butter, melted
1 egg, beaten
80g black treacle (or use molasses or golden syrup)
natural yoghurt, to serve

Preheat the oven to 180°C. Line a 20cm cake tin, including the sides, with baking paper.

Melt the butter and sugar together to form a syrup. Pour into the lined cake tin, then place the pears in the syrup, covering the base.

In a separate bowl, sieve all the dry ingredients including the second measure of sugar together and combine well. Stir in the milk, melted butter and egg to combine. Lastly add the treacle, and mix. Pour the mixture carefully over the pears until all covered.

Bake for 30–40 minutes, until a skewer inserted into the centre of the cake comes out clean.

Let the cake stand for 10 minutes, then turn out of the tin onto a serving plate, with the layer of pears on top. Serve with natural yoghurt.

Walnut, Prune and Apricot Slice

Whoever gave this recipe to me gave it two ticks. It certainly deserves them. In the country, you're always being asked to take a slice along to a gathering, and this one is always well received. It also freezes well.

½ cup sugar
1 cup flour
1 cup coconut
1 tsp baking powder
100g butter, melted
1 cup chopped prunes
1 cup chopped dried apricots
1 cup chopped walnuts
395g can sweetened condensed milk

Preheat the oven to 180°C. Line a sponge-roll tin with baking paper.

Combine the sugar, flour, coconut, baking powder and butter in a bowl then press into the tin. Bake for 10 minutes.

Remove from the oven and top with the dried fruit and nuts in a single layer. Drizzle over the condensed milk to evenly coat the fruit. Return the tin to the oven and bake for a further 20 minutes, or until golden.

Remove from the oven and leave to cool in the tin. Cut into squares when cold.

Keeps for at least a week.

Mouse's Gluten-free Apple and Blueberry Shortcake

There's always a guest these days who's gluten-free or has issues with their diet. I've tried this shortcake on a friend who is gluten intolerant, and she loves it. This slice is best served the day after baking.

250g peeled and cored Granny Smith apples
2 heaped tbsp gluten-free custard powder
160g butter
150g sugar
2 eggs
1 cup almond meal or ground almonds
1½ cups rice flour
2 tsp gluten-free baking powder
2 tsp guar gum (optional)
½–1 cup frozen blueberries
icing sugar, for dusting

Preheat the oven to 180°C. Grease a deep-sided slice tin.

Cut the apple into bite-sized pieces and cook in 1 cup water until tender and a little mushy.

Mix the custard powder to a paste with 2 tablespoons water, then add to the apple and cook to thicken. Remove from the heat and cool until no longer steaming.

Cream together the butter and sugar. Beat in the eggs. Sift in the almond meal, rice flour, baking powder and guar gum. Beat well. If the mixture looks a little wet, add a bit more rice flour. If dough is too soft to roll, chill in the fridge for 15 minutes.

Turn the dough out onto a floured board and cut in half. Press half of the dough into the prepared slice tin, reserving the other half for the top.

Spread the cooled apple mixture evenly over the top, then poke the still-frozen blueberries throughout the apple mixture. Roll the reserved dough out and place on top of the apple. This can be done in two pieces, as the dough is very soft.

Bake for 30–35 minutes or until the top is lightly browned.

Leave to cool completely before cutting into large slices. Dust with icing sugar to serve.

Lemon Tart

People love lemon tart for dessert; that's why it's often on restaurant menus. We've planted plenty of lemon trees at Te Parae so we can keep making this favourite forever.

1 quantity of shortcrust pastry (see page 239)
6 free-range eggs
250g caster sugar
zest and juice of 3 large lemons
200ml cream
icing sugar and double cream, to serve

Preheat the oven to 200°C.

Line a 26cm tart tin with pastry and bake blind for 20 minutes. Remove from the oven and reduce the heat to 160°C.

While the pastry is cooking, beat the eggs and sugar until well combined. Stir in the lemon zest and juice, then beat in the cream.

Pour the lemon mixture into the pastry case and bake until set, about 35–40 minutes. Remove from oven and leave to cool.

Dust with icing sugar before serving with double cream.

Japonica Apple and Orange Jelly

3kg japonica apples
6 large oranges
sugar (for quantity, see recipe method)

Wash and halve the japonica apples, including the skin and cores. Put all the japonica apples into a non-reactive saucepan (i.e. non-aluminium). Peel and slice the oranges, removing all the white pith. Add the oranges, cover with water and simmer for an hour, or until all the fruit has mushed down.

Pour all the juice and pulp into a muslin bag, suspend over a bowl and leave to drain overnight. Do not press or squeeze the bag, or the jelly will be cloudy.

Next day, discard the fruit from the muslin, measure the strained liquid and add an equal quantity of sugar. Bring the sugar and liquid slowly to the boil in a large, non-reactive pan, stirring once or twice until the sugar has dissolved. Skim off any foam that rises to the surface. Increase the heat and boil briskly.

Test for setting after 10–15 minutes by placing a little jelly on a cold saucer: if it sets, the jelly is ready. Pour the jelly into hot, sterilised jars and seal.

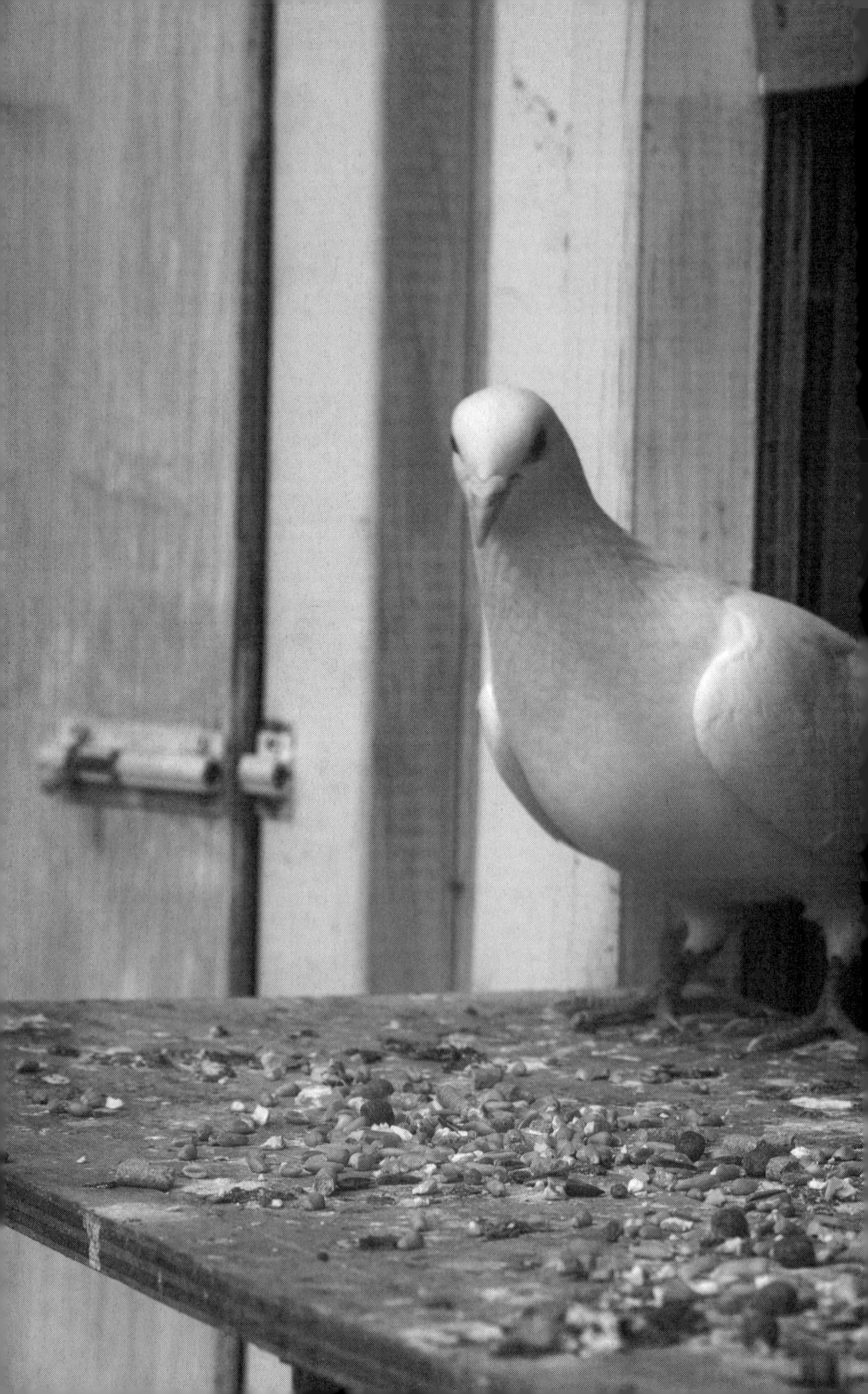

Te Parae poems

Ted Ferguson was head stockman for my grandfather, Alister Williams. His wife Hilary wrote this heartfelt verse about Te Parae, which summed up how so many people became attached to the homestead.

THE HOMESTEAD

What are the cords which bind this place
Close to our hearts with bonds of joy and pain?
The strands of heritage
Close woven in the warp and woof,
The very fabric of our being,
The very pattern of our family life,
Imposed upon a house and its surrounds
To make it Home!

The trees, which through a
    century of time,
Have blessed the sun and bowed
To storm of wind and rain,
Yet bowing did so seldom
    break,
But raised their woody arms
    again to God
In praise and supplication.
The trees whose leafy shade
Has many a whispered secret overheard,
Whose sturdy boughs supported
Tiny birds and romping child alike
With equal love,

And yet their dignity maintained.
And stately stand beside the
    smooth green lawns.
Within that garden, roses bloom
And paeonies, the like of which
    you have only dreamed,
While flags and water lilies
    wave and dip
Along the fringe of the lagoon.

Crowning the hill, the old house stands,
Eye-windows shining,
Content with the familiar scene
Of garden, trees and water spread
To meet the rolling lands
Of pastured flock and lowing herd;
While near at hand
The busy sounds of stable life
Salute the air.

Long have the gracious timbers,
    creeper-strewn,
Warmed to the welcome host
    and guest alike,
Have sheltered joy and gladness,
    grief and pain,
And ask no more than to remain their haven.

For people make the spirit
    of a home,
From them derives the thoughtful love,

The welcoming hand, the honest hope
That brews the essence of its fragrance
Clothed only by the things which give it visual form.
So it transpires, where e're they live,
These gentle folk may build again
Another refuge where the
    weary rest,
Another gracious house in comely garden set,
    Another Home!

Ted Ferguson was so moved by his time at Te Parae that he and his wife, Hilary, penned this poem about my grandfather, Alister Williams.

THE BOSS MAN
A man of stature
And of depths unsounded;
As the deeps of ocean surge and toss
*   or calmly flow*
Bearing great ships upon its crest
While cradling the tiny shell,
*   fragile, defenceless,*
So was he profound;
*   Courageous in adversity,*
*   Considering in perplexity,*
*   Rampant in the face of wrong*
*   and just;*
*   Couched in kindliness for*
*   The weak and wayward,*
*   Cutting to the crass but always*
*   courteous.*
Born of a noble line
Of England's best
And nurtured in her halls of
*   learning,*
He yet could meet the common
*   man*
On equal ground
And sweat beside him

In the fields of work, or sport,
    or war,
And still retain his own
    integrity;
    Intrepid champion,
    Implacable foe,
    Incorrigible raconteur,
    Whose silver tongue
      Turned incidents of moment
      To a tale of mirth and worth
      And hugely entertaining.
What can one say
Aught else of such a very
    human man,
But that we saw him as
    A generous master,
    A wise innovator,
    A proud father,
    A constant husband
    And were privileged
    To call him friend.

—With thanks, Ted and Hilary Ferguson

When I was cleaning out some stuff at Te Parae I came across this poem. It was apparently written in the nineteenth century and was used in the early 1920s by the New York Police Department. It is still recited today at many horse clubs and groups. Some of the language is archaic — for instance 'glanders and farcy' were fatal respiratory and skin diseases that were eradicated in the United Kingdom in 1928, and 'blinders' is an American word for 'blinkers'. Also, docking tails is no longer legal. Nonetheless, the sentiments still hold true for all horse lovers.

THE PRAYER OF A HORSE

To Thee My Master, I offer my Prayer.
Feed me, water me and care for me,
And when the day's work is done, provide me with shelter, a clean dry bed and a stall wide enough for me to lie down in comfort.
Talk to me. Your voice often means as much to me as the reins.
Pet me sometimes that I may serve you more gladly and learn to love you.
Do not jerk the reins and do not whip me when going up hill.
Never strike, beat or kick me when I do not understand what you mean,
but give me a chance to understand you.
Watch me, and if I fail to do your bidding,
see if something is not wrong with my harness or my feet.
Examine my teeth when I do not eat.
I may have an ulcerated tooth, and that, you know, is very painful.

*Do not tie my head in an unnatural position
or take away my best defence against flies or mosquitos by cutting off my tail.
And finally, Oh! My Master, when my useful strength is gone,
do not turn me out to starve or freeze,
or sell me to some cruel master to be slowly tortured and starved to death;
but do Thou, My Master, take my life in the kindest way,
and your God will reward you here and hereafter.
You may not consider me irreverent if I ask this in the name of Him who was born in a stable.
Amen*
—Author unknown

Select bibliography

Auckland Institute and Museum Online Cenotaph, www.aucklandmuseum.com/war-memorial/online-cenotaph

Fitzgerald, Caroline (ed.), *Letters from the Bay of Islands: The Story of Marianne Williams*, Penguin Books, 2004.

Godley, John R. (ed.), *Letters from Early New Zealand by Charlotte Godley 1850–1853*, Whitcombe & Tombs, 1951.

Hedley, Alex and Gareth Winter, *In the Boar's Path: Brancepeth*, Hedleys Books, 2012.

Hutt Valley Biographical Index and Genealogies, www.hbig.gen.nz

King, Michael, *The Penguin History of New Zealand*, Penguin Books, 2003.

Leonforte, Éric and Pierre Pujalet-Plàa, *One Hundred Legendary Trunks: Louis Vuitton*, Abrams, 2010.

Mason, Fergus, *Vuitton: A Biography of Louis Vuitton*, BookCaps, 2015.

McIntyre, Roberta, *The Canoes of Kupe: A History of Martinborough District*, Wairarapa Archive/Fraser Books, 2012.

New Zealand Weekly News, 21 July 1965, Wilson & Horton.

Papers Past, paperspast.natlib.govt.nz

Platts, Una, *Nineteenth Century New Zealand Artists: A Guide & Handbook*, Avon Fine Prints, 1980.

Sharp, C. A. (ed.), *The Dillon Letters 1843–1853*, A. H. & A. W. Reed, 1954.

Stephenson, Sharon, 'Town Mouse, Country Mouse', *NZ Life & Leisure*, Issue 58, November/December 2014.
Te Ara: The Encyclopaedia of New Zealand, www.teara.govt.nz
Wevers, Lydia, *Reading on the Farm: Victorian Fiction and the Colonial World*, Victoria University Press, 2010.
Williams, T. C., *A Letter to The Right Hon. W. E. Gladstone: Being An Appeal on Behalf of the Ngatiraukawa Tribe*, J. Hughes, 1873.